C000263004

COME
THEN GO AWAY

GERRY KING

⟨Tangent Books

Come Back To Me Then Go Away
First published 2021 by Tangent Books

Tangent Books
Unit 5.16 Paintworks, Bristol BS4 3EH
0117 972 0645
www.tangentbooks.co.uk
richard@tangentbooks.co.uk

ISBN 978-1-914345-08-1

Author: Gerry King

Cover design: Jaz Naish

Production and editor: Sol Wilkinson

Typography: Joe Burt

Publisher: Richard Jones

Overcoat Photo credit: Sophie P

A CIP record of this book is available at the British Library.

Printed on paper from a sustainable source

Printed by TJ Books Limited

Dedicated to my daughter Alexi

Would you like to know the score right now?
Well, I can't do that.
I cannot furnish you with details regarding people, places, or
things
until you have given me a little trust.

You see I'm a touch shaky to start.

And have you ever noticed when the timing needs adjustment
how the bonnet trembles on a thin-skinned Toyota?

Trust is a big word, longer than love.
The word nostalgia covers a greater spatial area than love or trust.
However, collectively love and trust contain just as many letters
as nostalgia.

Gerry King ©

CONTENTS

BATTERSEA TO *DANGER MAN* BY
WAY OF CHURCHILL'S FUNERAL

LOOKING FOR MONEY that doesn't exist anymore, in a car long crushed, parked on a street long demolished and waiting for my dad, now long gone. Orkney Street, Battersea, London SW11, recalling half a century, refracted through the quarterlight of an old motor, into the era of the smartphone, *Love Island* and threaded eyebrow influencers. Orkney evokes high angular German dreadnoughts; hazy, Mervyn-Peakish caped ghosts at Scapa Flow circa 1918 – steam punk without the chrome and studs. A memory of towering tenements, bomb sites half a decade after the Clean Air Act, and stock-footage street scenes recognized eons later in the black and white images of the Swiss American photographer Robert Frank. A gloomy street bereft of sun; doorsteps with H-shaped, cast-iron boot scrapers; china-handle coal scuttles; pianos in the basement; crates of beer brought back from *The Duke of Cornwall*; and uncles with bloodied trick fingers bedded down on cotton wool in matchboxes. This street was home to one of the South Coast Raiders, the forerunners of the Great Train Robbers. Sometimes concealing themselves in mail bags, these guys would steal high-value packages from the guard's cage, mostly on the Brighton line. I'd see the lamps with their frilly shades on the tables through the window of the first-class Pullman car as the train passed by the railing enclosure next to The Duke. I wonder now if a Raider toasted a snifter to the passing purse after a nice touch. I'm a child sitting on the front bench seat of a bulbous-nosed Vauxhall Vanguard, a vehicle with the aerodynamics of a brick. The column-change gear stick pokes out from the side of an unyielding steering wheel that would crush a rib cage like sugar frosted sponge fingers upon impact.

Dad has gone up the stoop into Nan's – my mum's mother – and I'm outside going through the glove box for 12-sided threepenny bit coins. "Stay with the car and lock the doors". I'd heard it so many times in early 1960s London. Dad was a self-employed refrigeration engineer at this time and there was always a stash of coins in the glove box for phone calls.

"Mister we'll watch yer car for a tanner," kids on the street used to shout. Knowing Dad, he probably gave them the sixpence. He could be kind and was good at walk-on parts, an initial impression – a bit of a charmer. However, sometimes the front would crack revealing the insecurities, frustration, and fears, that could ignite buried trauma, fanning out in red and lighting up the room.

As soon as the front door slammed, I was out of the car into the corner shop buying a Jamboree bag for thruppence. There were also custard creams in glass-topped square tins sold by the weight. Getting the goodies, the coloured, chalk sweets in the Jamboree bags along with a cheap novelty that made the naffest Christmas cracker seem luxurious; then back to the sanctuary of the motor, the cracked leather seats, pressing the lock stalks down, sitting behind the steering wheel… pretending. I spent so much time with my dad in cars and vans, waiting alone while he carried out his refrigeration work or visited suppliers. I remember the first watch Dad's mother, Nanny Joan, bought me – it was an Ingersoll. She had an Irish boyfriend called Garret, a coachman at Buckingham Palace, who ended up in a grace-and-favour flat at Windsor Castle. These were the days of cold cars and vans, bump starts, lingering condensation, and the smell of toast, damp, oil and leather. There was a sense of relief being invited into warm homes – it was like an acceptance. I was getting bad press even then. I suppose I was an overactive child, a mischief-maker. *Oh, he can be a handful...* The word mischief made me think of bandits because I always interpreted 'chief' as neckerchief and I didn't know my alphabet until I was 16 and couldn't spell 'hospital' until well into my twenties.

Years later, it was evident my dad was a philanderer, but then I just waited outside, never quite knowing the score. Some memories stick. I was in a long corridor in a plush West End mansion block, a short walk from Harrods, the type of place Dirk Bogarde, the 'Idol of the Odeon', would end his days. Concertina lift doors, the black mesh cage, polished brass and dark wood. I remember playing with a performing poodle – I've always noticed their dirty eyes – that could walk on its hind legs. Memories like a jazz score, weaving all over the place. One night, in the East End, we'd broken down, probably getting spares from the refrigeration suppliers Danfoss. I have a memory of being in a garage where there was a basket of Alsatian puppies. Another day going up the Monument, the site of the Great Fire of London, Dad telling me years later he carried me up. Maybe that's why I walked up the Statue of Liberty to the observation platform in 1969 while Dad's sister Edna and her husband Brian took the lift. They had a white toy poodle called Charlie; I think I was unkind toward it... But New York City was a decade away. The big old houses in Notting Hill; the Powis Square of Nicolas Roeg's *Performance* with Fox and Jagger; the West Indian families; high ceilings and everything in one room. I wonder if any were tenants of Peter Rachman. I met a lot more people in different environments than most kids of my age. I should have been confident, but it kept getting knocked.

Warriner Gardens was our first home. Mum and Dad had a flat there, between Battersea Park Road and Prince of Wales Drive. Richard Burton as Vic Daikin in the 1971 film *Villain* had a flat in Battersea Park Mansion; he'd park his 3.5 Rover Coupé outside and then drive his dear old mum down to the seaside for the day. I have sketchy memories of Warriner Gardens – things I was told, stuff that stayed with me. There was some violence associated with my mum's brother Uncle H and an Italian; it could've been within the family as H's wife was part Italian. A significant memory is of Trevor, a little boy who would have been my age. A friend of his dad's took him out one day in his van, a short-nose Bedford with sliding doors. I think the guy was a carpet fitter. Trevor ran across a road and was knocked down and killed. Sometimes, years later, I'd get a taste in my mouth, especially if I'd exerted myself, and it always reminded me of Trevor.

Later our family moved to Thornton Heath, Beverstone Road, where there was a cherry tree in the garden. I was playing with my toy fort in front of the black-and-white television when we heard President Kennedy had been assassinated in Dallas, Texas, November 1963. Sabu the elephant also died during the Beverstone Road period – I heard that from the top of the stairs. Dad had two lock-ups on Colliers Water Lane where he stored his Tedelex spares. During that time I was always with Dad because when we moved to Thornton Heath my brother Ian was born in Mayday Hospital, Croydon, February 1962. The reality was Mum's health was fragile. I remember her as petite at best and frail in later years. She'd had TB as a young woman and been in the Royal Brompton, a hospital that specialized in respiratory diseases. The Brompton cocktail, named in honour of the institution, was a mixture of heroin, cocaine, alcohol and Thorazine. It was an almost poetic elixir given to terminally ill patients 'to relieve pain and promote sociability near death'. I remember as a child seeing the angry scar on Mum's back where they'd removed part of her lung. She always felt too fragile to hug as I got older, and sometimes when a display of affection was required I didn't know what to do. Whole generations scarred by illness and war, making do and making it up as they went along; recipes staying the same, tips from the *Daily Mirror*, *Woman's Own* and the *Reader's Digest* slipping in along with barbiturates and slimming pills.

Culinary memories start at Beverstone Road, Dad cooking what he called scallops. These were thick wedges of potato, deep-fried in a mesh basket and served up with HP brown sauce. This would have been directly after Mum came home from the hospital. 'Cook's Tea' was a legacy of his National Service days – tea made with Carnation milk – a favourite because of the sweetness. Many years later, I would read books by B.S. Johnson and Julian Maclaren-Ross relating to army life, to gain some insight as to what National Service was all about and what the old man had experienced. Sunday joints usually turned into mince on Monday but in summer the beef was sliced and served with mashed potato and Branston pickle. The traditional fare would continue throughout the week, liver in thick gravy with onions and stew with butter beans and barley. Afters or desserts were bananas and Bird's custard, macaroni and rice puddings made with full-fat milk and topped with nutmeg. A treat would be scraping and eating the melted and burnt-by-degrees golden crust from the French Pyrex.

Vauxhall market, Sunday morning: Dad had a pitch in front of a café where he sold small fridges popular for bedsits and he made good money. The woman from the café used to take me upstairs into her front parlour, a room circled with porcelain-faced dolls staring down from a ledge. I always felt as if I'd been taken hostage in that room. *He's such a polite young man.* In the market there were brass Indian fancy goods and men who threw baskets of china in the air and told you how much they weren't asking. I loved the spiel. I'd wander about buying and scoffing huge slabs of fruitcake with my radio over my shoulder, the white wire of the earpiece twisted à la Johnny Ray.

The fridges were moved about, sitting upright to attention in order to keep the gas in the pots stable, in a military green Morris JB van with an almost cartoonish frog face. The van had previously been used to ferry scrambler motorbikes around and I'm sure had stickers for Redex on the sliding windows. The engine was in the cab between the front seats and it kept us warm, always smelling of hot oil, the padded sacking like a horse blanket over the engine cover. I could never imagine this van as new and wherever Dad parked it up local kids would get in and play. That van served him well. He eventually sold it to a chicken farmer near Caterham.

The vocabulary of fridges, the technical terms – I still look at fridge motor pots and think of windings, CO_2 and flux. I see the harelipped cutting tool going around the copper pipes and think of thermostats. I've always regarded fridges with affection. A delivered fridge had to be installed, which required letting it stand to allow the gas to settle. Fridges were a default setting for Dad, there was always money to be made with fridges: "You can always make a few quid if you've got a van, son".

Years later in Torquay, he had a gun-metal grey Mark 10 Jag and we'd go around the back of *Rumbelows*, an electrical store, looking for thrown-out trade-in fridges that we'd bung on the back seat. Over the years, I'd spend long nights sitting in various kitchens strung out on speed and listening to the pulsing drone of a fridge with the motor clicking on and off. If I had a fridge delivered now, I would still let the gas settle, to honour the memory.

Edging out to Surrey, we moved to South Godstone, Easter Way. 'Michelle' by the Beatles was the soundtrack of this time. Our house had a garage, a crab apple tree, a rockery, and chains swaged between brick pillars in the front garden. Later, a gate was cut in the back fence to the neighbours Marilyn and Laurie's house, who were to end up in a winter let in Pevensey Bay. Laurie worked in a bank. Marilyn was to throw her wedding ring on the fire and Laurie burnt a rug getting it out. One morning, I was to burn down a latticed wooden fence. I had made some toast in the eye-level grill, but I couldn't see my baby brother's nappies lying on top. I threw the nappies, smoking and burning, out of the back door where they landed near the fence. I was only trying to help.

Near the local pub, The Railway, there were a couple of small factories, and round the back of their workshops was a pit where they dumped what I assume were the seconds, items such as wall-mounted gas fire filaments that looked like beige biscuit waffles. Another factory used to throw out surgical waste and I remember the syringes. Somehow, my friends and I got it into our heads that buried at the bottom of the pit were dinosaurs and we would conjure up the fear among us around possible resurrection and related scenarios. There would have been commando sorties deep into enemy territory. I'd been given an explorer's kit as a Christmas present; it had a torch with different coloured filters, a safari hat, and a compass. Maybe it's all the same now but just different, every generation thinking they had the best fashion, music, cars and films. But what about the war years?

The acceptable face of war comes to the high street cinema and provides a fantasy for all those men who narrowly missed the call-up papers. I know my dad did – he told me. But he didn't fancy Korea. The screaming Stuka dive bomber, morphing into the glamorous armouries of an Ian Fleming-inspired cold war, complete with dinner-jacketed Whitehall-endorsed killers, playing the tables in casinos owned by men who had private zoos. DB6 Aston Martins, as opposed to North African desert patrol V8 Chevrolets piloted through Libyan deserts by fly-eyed, mesh-goggled, keffiyeh-wrapped wild men, steering by the stars and surviving on plunder. The Nazi Tiger tanks manoeuvred by Hugo Boss-uniformed Panzer aces sporting 'schmitte' duelling scars spinning doughnuts in pub car parks. Weird between-times – between rationing and Roy Orbison. I had the Corgi toys and the Commando comics plus swopsies war surplus, an officer's leather belt with brass loops and a canvas khaki-coloured gas-mask bag.

There was a television series during the 1960s called *Danger Man,* starring Patrick McGoohan as John Drake, a suave secret agent. He spoke in clipped tones, staring off to the side, constantly distracted. I spotted a car parked outside The Railway that was similar to the one he had driven in the series, a two-tone Simca Aronde. He was forever being chased around mysterious Eastern Bloc countries by villains like the Polish actor Vladek Sheybal, master of the meaningful stare. There was always accordion music played by men with magnificent moustaches, the women modelling flouncy lace blouses, and pencil skirts with wide belts fastened tightly round their waists. Village buildings were adorned with the painted signs of Vermouth and Pernod and someone was always reading a newspaper either in the Taverna or on the village square. Sometimes there would be elements of being captured and tied up. I found this quite titillating and liked a bit of that in my 'let's pretend', a step up from doctors and nurses. I was probably into the Japanese form of art bondage, Shibari, without knowing it.

The Railway was where Dad had a drink with the comedian Tony Hancock, and I would have crisps and coke in the beer garden. Tony Hancock committed suicide in Australia, but it didn't stop me following *Skippy the Bush Kangaroo*. My school was St Stephens C of E in Hunters Chase and I remember a girl whose dad was in the British Armed Forces in the Rhine. They owned a Ford Taunus. I had a cunning plan to secretly plant an orchard of apple trees in the school playing field using the pips from my fruit, but I just didn't have the knowledge, or probably the patience. Marilyn and Laurie, the rug burners, lived on Hunters Chase and I would go and watch the *Blue Peter* of John Noakes and Valerie Singleton in the house of a school friend, who also lived in the same street. I placed a waterproof coat in the bottom of a slatted fruit box to go sailing in the local stream – not a good idea. That box probably came from Spitalfields fruit and vegetable market. I live just around the corner now. Time refracted, degrees of separation.

January, 1965. A really early start; we drove from South Godstone to the funeral of Winston Churchill. Marilyn, the fiery wedding ring woman, came along with us – I never thought anything of it at the time. Standing in the cold near St Pauls Cathedral, drinking sweet tea and whiskey from a thermos kept in a duffel bag, I probably learnt the terms 'gun carriage' and 'pallbearer'. At six foot five inches, General de Gaulle was pointed out to me. Freddie Mills, 1940s world light heavyweight champion, and de Gaulle, connecting through the Citroen DS with its unique hydropneumatics. On the way back, Dad stopped at Caterham for 'a rest' with Marilyn, mere miles from home. Small details embedded before sleep on a big Vauxhall bench seat.

There is a black and white photograph by Austrian exile Wolfgang Sushitzky, taken in August 1942 from a heightened vantage point at St Paul's Cathedral. The photograph depicts the flattened bomb devastation from the cathedral to the City of London in the east. The bullet and blast scars, and pitted shrapnel, are still evident in the stonework of St Paul's and Tate Britain at Millbank. I noticed the same type of scars in 2018 that are now being filled in and covered over on buildings in Berlin's Museum Island. Erasing the past through restoration.

I recall playing on post war Battersea bomb-sites, like the ones in Don McCullin's early photographs, when we used to visit my cousins in Tulse Hill. There were always old cars with running boards and bulky mudguards – alongside broken prams, the small wheels of which were removed for go-karts. Scammell trucks, that once used to pull army tanks, were pulling rows of terraced houses down with cables attached to winches. Price's Candles factory, the smell of tallow, and Arding & Hobbs at Clapham Junction, just down the road from Oswald Mosley's one-time fascist café meeting place, where a contrived, old, dishevelled Etonian Mayor held a broom like a redundant wizard after the riots in 2011.

On one particular visit, Mum and Dad went up to granddad Harold's flat in Tilbury Court while I waited outside in the motor. Maybe I was just too much trouble, too hyperactive, for the recently bereaved. My grandmother Lillian had died, and Mum washed her ready for the undertakers. I looked in the wing mirror, saw a cloud and thought it was Nan. I remember Mum drawing the curtains one sunny afternoon for a young girl who had died of meningitis, as her funeral cortege came down our road. Timing, awkwardness – when does the laughter respectfully start again?

My dad first visited Nanny Lil at Orkney Street. My mum's younger brother was called Harold and Dad had met him during National Service in the army. I can imagine Dad going into the house with Harold.

Come on in, Paul, meet the family… This is my dad.

Pleased to meet you, Mr Vigor.

No need for that boy, call me Harold. Pull up a chair, sit down and have a cup of tea. Come on girls, make yourself scarce…

Maybe that's when Dad first met my mum, Greta – apparently named after the Swedish actress Greta Garbo. The eldest of the three daughters, she had passed her school certificate and was working in the typist pool of Morgan Crucible, a company developing the properties of carbon in components for search lights and cinematic equipment.

Families. Dad's own family had consisted of his mum, grandmother and sister. During the war, Dad's father was captured by the Japanese at the fall of Singapore. He was to survive the Death Railway and bring my dad home a pair of crepe-soled Japanese infantry boots. In the late forties, Granddad emigrated to New Zealand, after a stopover and another marriage in Canada. Dad's mother and sister emigrated to America in the 1950s. It was as if everyone was on the run.

Bad brakes on the Vauxhall estate coming down to the Purley Way marked the end of our Surrey days. The bonnet of our car slid under the back of a flatbed articulated truck. There would have been no seatbelts – Dad threw his arm across my brother and me. The self-employed refrigeration business went out the window. Car accidents and compensation. During the 1990s, Dad would get more than 70 grand from another motor accident and my brother over 100 grand – but it didn't do either of them any good.

The Vauxhall had been serviced; the brakes had been bled but the fluid had not been replaced. Dad's arm across us, the same arm that delivered countless blows against all comers on an Anderton and Rowland boxing booth across the south of England, until he turned professional in the early 1950s. The breaks he never had, two extremely significant fights that determined his destiny, two fights and a bad one-eyed manager Jack Turner, whose claim to fame was fighting the illustrious Sunderland-based Cast Iron Casey in the 1930s. Dad's southpaw move, his arm holding us back, was to be significant, setting up the next move down to the South West. The only problem with moving to another place is that you take yourself with you. The dislocated shoulder injury was to be the precursor to the relocation, the fourth move in nine years. A gentle graduation, within what was to be the M25 orbit, out of London proper and then finally hurtling down to Torquay where

Dad had grown up. This accident on the Purley Way was when the metaphorical clutch was engaged and much of what followed was freewheeling.

Bad breaks or bad decisions, Dad isn't here anymore for me to ask. I can only put the pieces together and the memories that come back are like voice-overs in Ealing comedies and 1950s film noir thrillers with severe women like Barbara Stanwyck, while the men are George Cole, Sid James and Robert Mitchum. Everything connected to changing the way you feel: a movie, the TV, a comic, being alone eating sweets in a car waiting for Dad, to the later adult chemical cloak of my own Zorro.

Neil Young sang about buying a pickup and moving to L.A. Ours wasn't a brave enough move, it was really just a neutral corner, a mere distraction when real change would require serious effort. Kids get excited, adults get anxious. This was my dad's easy option, the romanticism of a conquering hero, a homecoming never quite deserved. Drinking with his pals, the self-deprecating jokes, referring to himself as 'Canvas Back King'. He was talented – there is no doubt about that – but he was wasted. Nothing lasts forever. The boxing kit branded Everlast certainly doesn't relate to the mortals that wear it.

A Pickfords removal van took us to Devon and we moved into a pub on a road that led to the sea. My bedroom on the first floor looked out at the illuminated Crown & Sceptre sign. There was a gym at the back of the pub – I was good on the speed and pea ball. I remember being taken to the local school and introduced again as the new boy like a character from a Penelope Lively short story. There was a post box in the outside wall of the school, and I would write letters and mail them to myself. For a while, it was all summer on the beach. Bizarrely, I don't remember a winter in that pub, but I do remember the gym being cold and the unique experience of having a pee in the public bar gents first thing in the morning, the stimulating smell of Jeyes fluid and the forced gushing of the urinal faucets.

From the thruppences out of the glove box in the Vauxhall Vanguard to the sixpences in the wire-meshed Dimple whisky bottle. Now playing for the three cherries jackpot on the pull-down handle fruit machine with its ratcheting clicks, spin and thunks. Taking yourself with you.

DISTRACTION NUMBER ONE

The letterbox snaps me back into the now like someone knocking at the door. Our bouffant-coiffured, blonde, Lithuanian postwoman, Victoria, has a habit of folding over the letters before she puts them through the door, causing the flap to snap back. Last week, I received a colour-saturated John Hine postcard of creased puffins from Cornwall. This is not a criticism of my postie; she has delivered thick tomes to me ordered through Abe Books – I feel guilty burdening her with the weight.

I had been contemplating desks and a trip that took me to a crematorium in Wadebridge, Cornwall, where my pal Nick the Grate, who had given me my first desk, was laid out in a wicker coffin. Nick had owned a fireplace shop near the Arches on Gloucester Road in Bristol called Grate Expectations. I had planned to go on an Arvon Poetry week and at that time I didn't have a bank account. I gave Nick the cash and he handed me a company cheque from Grate Expectations to send to the Arvon foundation. I didn't have a desk at the time, I lived in a shared house in Clifton and used the kitchen table.

John Hartley Williams and Matthew Sweeney were the Arvon writers in residence. Late night card games and red wine, an edgy middle-class decadence, a lesson in tolerance. I was gratefully exposed to the music of Tom Waits: *Swordfish Trombones*. On my return to Bristol, Nick dropped the desk round to where I lived but there was one drawer missing. He left it on the pavement when he loaded it up and when he went back it was gone. The desk was so big it had to be heaved through a large sash window.

I wrote some of my favourite poems on that desk – 'Without Love' and 'Without War'. I also completed an Access in Humanities Course, that enabled me to go to university. The work I did at that desk would change my circumstances and introduce me to a new circle of friends. I have had a trinity of desks from England and one from Wales. The second was a standard office desk, a graduating beige and probably surplus from a Devon Healthcare Trust. My brother Ian gave it to me, and it served me well, creating some short films and completing a PGCE.

The day of Nick's funeral I got a lift with a friend from Bristol to Wadebridge as I did not have faith in my black Saab with the dodgy diesel pump making it to Cornwall and back. An old guy once said to me on a petrol station forecourt, "Those motors eat themselves". He then went on to explain that some of the bearings in the engine are made of nylon. These grind up and finally destroy the diesel pump and when that goes it's game over. I spoke at Nick's funeral and returned to London to start a job working nights at a wet hostel on Cambridge Heath Road opposite Hurwundeki.

The third significant desk was discovered some years later in the vicar's office of a church in Bristol prior to my move to London. My friend Adam, a musician, was working as the caretaker in this church, and while we were discussing the terms of renting a room for rehearsals for a forthcoming performance at the Arnolfini with my pal Glenn, I noticed a brown box wood desk with a tatty leather top that sat on two pedestals with drawers. It was clearly not being used. I asked if it was for sale and was told it was mine for a donation. At the time, I was living around the corner from the BBC in Redland, Bristol, in a big, old Victorian pile with large bay windows. These buildings are a recurring theme in my life. The desk looked the part in my bedroom, sitting on my 70% lamb's wool ivory gold carpet, looking out on a granite fractured rockery.

When I eventually moved to London it was in an unusually wide-bodied van that was once used for carrying hang gliders. As we made our way up the M4, the driver told me he had lost his son in a hang-gliding accident a few years previously and couldn't bear to part with the van. He was stick-thin and I had noticed him, some months earlier, walking on rooftops near my girlfriend Louise's Georgian apartment that had roof issues and a disorganized management company. The roof needed some attention but there was no way they could afford scaffolding. The driver had walked her Georgian roof some weeks later, sorted the tiles out and when the time was ready, he drove the ecclesiastical desk and me to the East End of London.

Louise relocated from Georgian splendour to an old converted forge in South West Wales. It was agreed the desk would be more suited to her home than my 1920s tenement opposite the Jewish Soup Kitchen in Spitalfields, London. I wrapped it in old quilts, packed it into the back of my then reliable Saab and thundered down the M4 to the small town of Burry Port, a few miles from Llanelli, where Amelia Earhart, accompanying pilot Wilmer Stultz, came ashore in June 1928. Stultz was to die July 1st, 1929, after he crashed while intoxicated at Roosevelt Field in Mineola, New York.

The desk I'm now using is an old cream and pine trimmed Ikea piece that I bought from a YMCA shop in Swansea for £25. My 27-inch iMac is propped up to eye level on two books, Andy Warhol's *Giant* and David LaChapelle's *Heaven to Hell*. I'm writing this book on it. Nick the Grate also gave me an enamelled Warhol *Campbell's Soup* sign and a vintage ice bucket. I still have both.

BUCKINGHAM PALACE AND
HUGHIE GREEN'S TRAIN SET

THE PUB IN Torquay 1966 – *and all that*. Salvation and shame served up through St Marychurch, Church of England on Fore Street. I don't remember anything friendly or redeeming about any association with the church. The school I went to was church-affiliated, the headmaster a bent-fingered ex-cricketer, who had the most unattractive habit of picking his nose and eating it. He drove a two-tone blue, mark II Ford Consul. One Tuesday, he slippered me for being late to school and as a result I considered Tuesday an unlucky day for many years. However, he redeemed himself by reading *The Lion, the Witch and the Wardrobe* to our class on Friday afternoons. The nearest I came to experience any salvation was through this escapism.

The vicar caught a few of us kissing in his graveyard and told the headmaster, as if we'd done something really naughty. We were 10-year-olds. I remember the shame, standing in front of the headmaster, the solemnity of the situation. I'm sure our parents weren't involved, adding yet another unspoken dimension to a totally unnecessary situation. A disturbing fact is both the boys I was hauled in with were, as adults, convicted of rape.

The choirmaster, Mr. Subry, tried his best with a rabble of

boys who made up a song about him:

Ding dong, ding dong,
Subry's gone wrong.
What shall we do?
Lock him in the loo.

He wasn't really 'church' in the same sense as the collaborating bastards that were the vicar and headmaster, and he'd get us gigs at half a crown each for weddings. There were rumours involving camping weekends with a fiddling vicar who just happened to run the youth club. A husband and wife, who were straight out of the Grant Wood painting *American Gothic,* organized the scouting activities. They drove an olive-green split window-screen Morris 1000. As I recall, they were dour but decent people and I enjoyed Scouts. I went through a period of dressing up as a vicar, wearing a white polo neck under a cassock. Some years later I would add a black curly NHS wig my mother had been supplied with after her cerebral haemorrhage operation, and over the top, pull on a Second World War gas-mask. I'd jump out of the bushes or from behind hedges in the local park. Even though I wasn't Catholic and didn't have that obvious edge of theatricality, I think I would have made a really good Catholic for a number of reasons, particularly the colourful robes, the swinging brass thuribles of incense and the guilt and resolution through regular confession. The Catholic church St Denis was two streets away and had a pointy spire, a convent, and walled garden. The theatrics might have kept me in check but then I remember my dealings with the nuns and how I was invited into their kitchen and given tea and chocolate biscuits in return for a key to their garden gate I had somehow acquired. Many years later, I was to buy some small items of furniture from a jumble sale in this convent. I felt they wouldn't be tainted and somehow the pieces would retain a good energy.

The school, the church, Scouts and youth club – that was my orbit and it wasn't enough. I lived in a pub and one thing I remember is that all the individuals of authority in my life at this time never came near it. I'd identified something that I couldn't articulate.

At Scout camp in New Addington, Greater London, I watched a badger being skinned, suet power being rubbed between the pelt and the innards sac as the fur came off. My pal from school, John, was also at the camp and on our big day out in London he lost the 10-shilling note his mum had given him. We were trusted to go off by ourselves and to meet at some determined time at Baden Powell House. John's mother, Phyllis, who was always kind to me, had allegedly been the mistress of a Torquay bookmaker Bernard Redfern, the father of Anthea who was once married to Bruce Forsyth, host of the 1970s *Generation Game*.

Pre or post loss of John's 10 bob note, we found ourselves at Victoria station – there were huge billboards advertising *Ice Station Zebra*, a cold war spy thriller. We went into the cartoon cinema; there was still Pathé news then, which of course by today's standards would have been old news. How to entertain ourselves in London with very little money? I had the bright idea of going to Buckingham Palace to find my Uncle Garret, who had courted my grandmother. We rolled up, two Boy Scouts in uniform with our fleur-de-lis motif belts stamped 'Be Prepared'. I'd been to the guardsmen's entrance in Buckingham Palace Road with my dad some years before. We'd been in the social club there to meet Garret and have a cup of tea. At one point, a bearskin had been put on my head. This time I asked to see my Uncle Garret, who fortunately turned up and welcomed us in. I remember him showing us some of the Queen's horses, taking us around the stables and to where the Coronation coach was stored. We were probably hoping he'd drop us a few bob but that didn't happen and, knowing now what tight arses the royal family are, I can understand on his wages. When we finally met up with the rest of the troop at Baden Powell House, nobody believed we'd been to Buckingham Palace. My mum kept the souvenir glasses I'd bought her in the cocktail cabinet for many years, little tankards with famous London scenes. Fifteen years later, they went when it all went, when Mum and Dad split up just before her death and the house was sold.

Kids in those days didn't knock about with their mum and dad. I didn't, and I don't remember much about my brother either during this time. At night, I would sneak out of the pub through the stable door at the back, catch the bus downtown and wander about – no one would miss me. I don't say that with self-pity, it was a good thing as I wouldn't get told off. There was a model railway on show in the old town hall next to the synagogue on Abbey Road. The railway belonged to the TV presenter Hughie Green, who always came across as a dodgy salesman with his catchphrase, "Most sincerely, folks". It later transpired he was the father of Paula Yates, a successful morning TV presenter, who was once married to the pop star Bob Geldof. I was fascinated by the detail of the display; the models, the tunnels, and trains. It was the element of order that appealed to me, knowing the train would come around again. My dad used to take me to an attraction in Battersea Park fairground. We would sit in a boat that floated, sloshing and creaking, through a dark tunnel, past lit dioramas of famous world landmarks set back in alcoves. This subdued and dimly lit trip around the world was very safe and controlled. There was no loud music. I knew where I was with it. There were elements of this safeness in the railway exhibition.

I would also spend time in the churchyard, the gravestones holding a fascination, especially the damaged and cracked ones. May 1943 the church had been bombed and 45 people died, mostly children, including some already orphaned by the war. The tombs and grave markers had been fractured. I would have been searching for skulls, but I never found any. I don't remember ever having a fear of the dark.

DISTRACTION NUMBER TWO

It is night and we are driving. Nick Cave's 'Higgs Boson Blues' is playing on the CD; the shimmery reds and greens of the dashboard complement the muted music. I'm sure Nick Cave drives a Jaguar and lives in Brighton. I like the way he performs on stage; I like his style, especially the way he uses his arms. The song name-checks Geneva but we're driving around Hartcliffe, a sprawling social housing satellite in Bristol, looking for a church hall where the 70th birthday party of an old pal is being held. An old pal who is significant. I remember years ago when he was running a white goods store selling fridges and cookers, he bought me a copy of *A Spaniard in the Works* by John Lennon. Our connection runs deeper than a gifted book and much longer than John was married to Yoko.

Hartcliffe – this once familiar working-class suburb, the 'homes fit for heroes' post-WWII – is an analogue story living on in a digital age. Heavy industry and tobacco factories are long gone but a mega-saviour supermarket spreads its largesse of zero-hour contracts around like a selective papal blessing.

The wide, almost-Parisian boulevards of Hartcliffe offer a turning circle in which two London cabs could perform a double circle in opposite directions. Behind me is a silver-grey Renault Espace with a lazy eye headlight. I pull over and let them pass while

35

Daughter phones her friend, who is already at the party, and asks for her location and postcode. "Don't you find technology overwhelming, Dad, everything changing so quickly?"

I then start to wonder – is it? And reply, "I try my best or ask you." The truth is I'm glimpsing a place where I'll never get through the door. It feels I've no business there.

I must have said it out loud, as Daughter says, "Where's that – the future?" Speaking my thoughts out loud – I keep doing that. It isn't really a problem, but it does become one when I say something critical or mildly offensive. I need to watch this, especially in the age of the easily offended with their penchant for virtue calling and their perceived entitlement. Is this the age of the coward?

The Daughter goes back to keying the postcode into her phone and a programmed voice tells us where to go and we believe them. In Houndsditch the other day I was buying stamps. As the postal worker handed them over, she said to me, "There you go, dear..." Even with my leather jacket, fingerless gloves and a swept-back, grey bouffant Paulie in The Sopranos would be proud of, I'm sinking in the quicksand of now. My shoulders and chest are firm with the anticipation of violence.

I recall a neck and shoulder massage above a chemist in South Wales, "Oh you've got a lot of tension in your neck..." Yes, of course I have. It's a by-product of my imposter syndrome and I'll be going down through the ceiling tonight using my James Smith umbrella to catch the plaster. Perceptions are changing and I'm not even sure how I want to be seen.

Cassettes were new in my youth and my first music was on vinyl. There was the fleeting appearance of eight-track cartridges, but they never really caught on. They looked raggedy before their time, living in cardboard sleeves with their peeled labels. What a let-down after covers like the Aubrey Beardsley-inspired Beatles album *Revolver* or *London Calling* by The Clash. Nobody ever skinned up on an eight track. Cassette case tapes might have been good for a toot. Analogue to digital, painterly to pixels. I realize my ears don't get the subtleties of high spec systems – I've probably got an analogue default setting courtesy of tinnitus.

Hyper clarity reminds me of a Stratford Westfield shopping experience when I decided to go to John Lewis to buy a digital radio for a birthday present. I found the whole place mesmerizing, the way the ground floor sloped ever so slightly, almost a natural incline, pulling you in. The bright lighting and sparkling mirrors highlighted my mature flaws of greying bushy eyebrows, skin blemishes and my off-white teeth giving a clue of an expensive dental plate. I find myself considering a Hungarian dental packaged holiday, recuperating holed up in a muted tonal hotel room with codeine, sparkling water and an android tablet loaded with Netflix boxsets. The consumer mentality starts hacking away like a relentless salesman. Arthur Miller would have nailed it and Marilyn Monroe would have been the face of L'Oréal. I start working out payments on things I don't need, like a new iMac. I conjure up David Bowie as *The Man Who Fell to Earth* – I feel alienated through spending power and my consumer ignorance. I am seduced by 0% interest and nothing to pay for 12 months. Machines that are a sealed unit, a real nightmare if anything goes wrong, unless of course you pony up for the extended cover. Then I remember the words of Kamal from the tech shop on Bethnal Green Road, "Old is gold". He explained to me that with the old iMac's you can just slam in a new hard drive and you're away again until they make the operating systems obsolete. Playing for time.

This is the age of agency, of management fees and never being clear of the supplier or service you bought into. Don't think about owning anything lock, stock, and barrel. Housing developments where you pay for the verges to be cut, the roads and lighting to be maintained, all on top of your council tax. Paying for the privilege to live on land that is no more than a corporate holding. Your life – their business. Mark E Smith ranted, "Your future – our clutter". Cars you never own, holidays you never pay off, spa breaks, little treats, big treats, LED lights in hairdressers' new kitchens, and a soundtrack provided by the auto-tuned Cher: *Believe.*

I have an A to Z in the car door pocket with a magnifying glass, but in future I will Google and get a suction holder for my mobile phone. Move with the times. A Chinese saying comes to mind: Tell me and I forget – show me and I remember. Daughter and I can sit in a room together quietly reading. I think this is something special. It wasn't always like this – there were times of trouble before she was born, when nothing felt comfortable, when no one felt right. When you got what you deserved.

It's cold because we're in November. I pull up outside the hall, the downward illumination of the opening car doors lights up the pavement like a scene from *Repo Man.* I want to live as long as Harry Dean Stanton, who smoked between his morning yoga stretches. A few people are outside the hall smoking and two young girls in fleecy dressing gowns, one wearing pink fluffy slippers, walk past, talking to each other and refreshingly not into mobile phones. A Japanese four-wheel drive with no one at the wheel is parked on a verge with its engine running. A man points a torch into a Ford Transit engine bay while another does something with spanners. It's a Saturday night and there is a sense of urgency, they probably want the motor up and running to do a Sunday market. Maybe it's an alternator or starter motor – it's an old-school Transit, mechanical. My car – an unusual, aubergine-black Saab diesel – is half and half; it can be plugged in for diagnostics but there is still a mechanical element in its build and it's getting on, certainly one of the motors the mayor of London wants to bury. The party will ebb and flow, there will be photographs and cake and no going back.

Do you notice the black ambulances, usually Mercedes, the body movers? I remember the morning when my dad died, and I was sitting talking to the matron in her office when the undertaker and his assistant took my dad out in a body bag. The bag sagged in the middle like the pouch of a black slingshot with handles at each end. I caught a glimpse and wanted to unsee it. My dad's sister had her back to the door, she didn't notice this event but then she lives in the States and they want to live forever. Auntie wears a big diamond and has had procedures. She's eighty-plus and you only know this when she moves. There is a block of offices at Bishopsgate near Liverpool Street station, for health and safety reasons it's entirely covered with fabric over the scaffolding, but they've gone one better and added a huge panel on the top depicting clear blue skies: the skies of a world out of this world, more *Blade Runner* than Brighton. Death and regeneration let's keep it under wraps. *Nothing to see here, now move on.*

I've got a head start with relative poverty. However, I want a cool longevity, respectable for my age, not a Photoshopped Iggy Pop fantasy, topless and ripped under a blazing blue Californian sky with static palm fronds, next to a black Bentley. I'd be happy with some London brick wall and my Aberdeen Crombie, some decent strides and city-shined shoes. Getting older is like the school report – must try harder. You need to put the effort in and I'm walking about breathing in diesel particles and can't afford a new motor. I'll be long gone when the Tesla is affordable, like a quality Volvo depreciating as it leaves the showroom.

On the very day the BBC reported that New Orleans piano player Fats Domino had died peacefully in his sleep aged 89, I had been to see the Ilya and Emilia Kabakov exhibition at the Tate Modern. Since my dad died 10 years ago, anyone through location, nationality, or gender, is now in my personal comparable mortality countdown. The last time I remember hearing about Fats Domino was during 2005 when hurricane Katrina struck New Orleans, flooding the Lower Ninth Ward where he lived (a predominantly working-class American Hartcliffe) and he had to be rescued by a coastguard helicopter from the roof of his home. I learnt the pioneering rock 'n' roll musician, famous for his Blueberry Hill number, had left school at 14 and had worked in a bedspring factory during the day and played piano in bars at night.

In 1985 Ilya Kabakov, a Russian artist, created 'The Man Who Flew into Space from His Apartment' in a Moscow studio. This was later to be part of a larger work, *Not Everyone Will Be Taken into The Future*, made in collaboration with his wife and partner Emilia. The work depicts a cramped room, a representation of a Soviet worker's home, equipped with a small bed, two wooden utility chairs facing each other, and a plank resting between which serves as a launch platform. The walls are covered in futurist style posters celebrating the Communist party and its leaders – cold war propaganda, always a promise of something other, something better, something later. Hanging from the ceiling is a homemade slingshot fashioned from bedsprings and canvas. The bed springs are attached to each corner of the canvas seat. Directly above the seat of the slingshot is a large, brightly lit hole in the ceiling where a man has launched himself into space – the star man pre-Elon Musk. Gimme that old time magical realism, tell me it's going to be alright. David Bowie is piloting a Tesla through space.

Getting older, getting away, getting out of it. Fats Domino never left his home State after 1986, not even to be inducted into the Rock and Roll Hall of Fame in NYC. It took a flood and a helicopter to move him and that was only to another part of his home state, Louisiana.

I had never really taken to science fiction. Space for me was brightly coloured tin ray guns with grinding flint wheels creating spark effects and the stilted speech of rocket man Dan Dare. I assumed the enunciation was a space thing. The actors operated in flat shaky sets up on the silver screen, usually with a droning soundtrack, shouting orders like, "Fire the thrusters now!" There never seemed to be a love interest in space, Carlo Ponti and Sophia Loren weren't orbit-swanning people.

There was a derelict Victorian villa near a cinema in Torquay and, after the ABC minors Saturday morning pictures, a few of us kids would go there and play. It was an enthralling place for a child, with an overgrown garden behind slightly shuttered gates, a straggly wild fig tree, assorted stunted fruit trees and naked plinths relieved of their statuary. We would climb up onto the crumbling patio and enter through the insecure French windows into a high-domed room. In the centre of the water-damaged parquet floor, its individual segments lifting and warping, sat a cylindrical rocket with its skyward pointy nose. It was a faded blue, a colour that would now adorn an Islington front door. We had to step over a lip to get inside and sit on a small shelf that started and ended either side of the entrance. There was a circular glass porthole halfway round this seating arrangement, in a prize position for the purpose of space exploration. Three or four of us would pile in and sit with knees touching, our dedicated sound-effected faces willing the jets we whooshed to take us away, the tapering white hot rockets thrusting us into the Guinness blackness. The rocket stood about eight feet tall, but it seemed huge, certainly big enough for our dreams. I can still smell the hardwood and damp and there were times in life I wished I was back in the spaceship. Back to Kabakov, the space-propelled Soviet worker escaping his overcrowded environment, the repressive regime and Fats Domino living in his small contented orbit amongst his community. Me, I'm just trying to get through this life knowing there is more time behind me than in front.

In the future, the skies are different, high definition images illuminate Times Square, New York City, Piccadilly, London and the pseudo-capitalist Beijing, while Macau serves as the Las Vegas of the orient, pollution providing a cloak of sulphurous shimmery yellow. Adverts flash for predominantly Middle Eastern flight providers and Far Eastern electronics. The blue-sky screens over the buildings are like the colourful wrapped Reichstags of the late conceptual artists Christo and Jeanne-Claude, recognizing the temporary nature of everything. It's there and it isn't – bytes of Ozymandias flickering in the desert. Coca-Cola is the real thing and Pepsi is good for stomach ache, but both are effective in cleaning chrome. I see the proliferation of sushi bars, the type of food Harrison Ford eats, as the character Rick Deckard, hunched in steam and neon. The Asian restaurants on Brick Lane are gently disappearing. These culinary conduits have served their purpose. The next generation will begin their careers in the offices of the City, not the kitchens.

On the corner of Hanbury Street, Brick Lane, London, I spy the octogenarian writer Clive Murphy, who has lived above a curry house since 1973. Clive is outside Dark Sugars, the artisan chocolate shop. Paul, the owner of this business, drives a vintage red Jaguar. Clive is steering a blue push-along stroller wearing a black Russian rabbit fur-lined ushanka hat and red braces under his overcoat. I know he's a royalist through previous heated exchanges in his two-roomed apartment. Clive is a man who works with what he's got and I have never known him to show any sense of self-pity. We stand talking and he asks me to reach into the stroller basket and throw an empty air freshener canister into a nearby bin. Clive is 35mm as opposed to digital, the flickering light between the frames, a respite from the streamed banality. He can be infuriatingly contrary, but then I realize much of this is probably down to living as a bachelor for many years – no filter so to speak. The naughty outbursts are usually concluded with a twinkle in his soulful blue eyes. His *Ribald Rhymes* series of poetry books, with titles such as *Lock Up Your Sons* and *Gay Abandon*, have gained some notoriety. He told me his editor-come-typist is not returning his calls. He thinks she has a drink problem.

However, while these slim volumes are mildly amusing, the books he'll be remembered for are about ordinary people he encountered while living in shared bedsit accommodation during the 1970s. The memoirs of a former chorus girl and a lavatory attendant, with titles such as *Love, Dears!* and *Four Acres and a Donkey.*

In Clive's work there is a Warholian 15-minutes-of-fame prolonged through the Chicagoan Studs Terkel page-ordered reportage – the minutiae of the everyday, the fabulously ordinary. Clive's output will be retained in the Bishopsgate Institute, lovingly catalogued by the fabulously monikered Stefan Dickers. Clive's entourage also includes his executor Patrick Wray, head of the fiction department at Foyles Charing Cross Road. Clive is a man who deserves attention. The first time I met him Dame Sian Phillips was reading an excerpt of his work at an event in the Bishopsgate Institute. He is a unique individual, essentially 'in living memory'. I leave Clive to continue his shopping, but he stays with me all day.

I swing over to Commercial Street, passing a neon heart in the window of Tracey Emin's local, a present to her friend the Hula Hooping Sandra, and cross at Christchurch Spitalfields to Toynbee Street, where development awaits the row of shuttered ghost businesses. In Brune Street, the matzos and tins of celery soup once distributed from the Jewish Soup Kitchen are now just a receding recollection in the memories of the few. Marion, in her nineties, a carer to her cousin in her late eighties, told me they are amongst the last three Jews (that she knows of) in the nearby Denning Point tower block.

In Artillery Passage, the cobbles now long covered, Ottolenghi's juts out of the corner. The galleried presentation of comestibles for the more discerning of appetites wouldn't be out of place over the road as an installation in Raven Row. I consider the distance to the nearest fatberg. The rats are a given, popping up through the drains on a regular basis. The new Fruit and Wool exchange opposite Spitalfields market abuts Whites Row and mops up land like man-spread on a packed Central Line tube. The ghost of a brutal NCP car park and a strip of Ripper killing ground are totally absorbed into the glass and chrome of the new emporium, the brick cladding rolled on like a rustic Fablon with snide stone trying it on until the pollution stains it, doing it a favour. The local demographics are changing. I'm imposing memories on new facades.

The world is changing and I'm trying to change with it. The university of the third age is in a classroom, but I want to stay out in the world, tramping the streets and riding the tube. I want to be that 'room for one more' as the doors close. The sweep and the swish, clang and thunder as I'm squeezed up against the door hurtling toward Bank and through to St Paul's. Sometimes sparks in the tunnel take me back to the El in downtown Chicago. I look out for book readers on the tube, I want the tide to turn like the acquittal of the Birmingham Six or the Guildford Four – sensationally, the impossible becomes a reality. Possible literary couplings for singletons through openly displayed reading material. Their phones in flight mode, their faces out of the digital screens.

On a bright, cold, blustery Sunday morning, I was running over Southwark Bridge listening to Dexys Midnight Runners on my iPhone. I made a celebratory noise as I yomped on; my feet swaddled in Smartwool socks encased in my Gortex Ecco Cheviot boots. Rejoicing in this physical feat, taken for granted in youth, I realized in that moment how lucky I was. The Millennium Bridge had been closed for the filming of yet another blockbusting entertainment involving Tom Cruise saving a portion of the world/humanity/small child or possibly a French bulldog. I started to unhealthily focus on Cruise when my tendonitis began playing up. I could see him waving from the chimney of the Tate Modern in a black outfit with what appeared to be membranes under his arms – of course he was harnessed. He must have a fabulous view of the Scientology building from up there – almost a Jesus on the cross moment, "Peter, I can see your house from here..." The dolphin-nosed camera helicopter flew backwards, sweeping and bowing like an aerial dancer.

There is a small private garden around the corner from

Shakespeare's Globe Theatre by the side of Tate. A pal of mine took me in there one lunchtime and I picked some thyme. I like the idea of this herb growing in close proximity to the river Thames and remember some obtuse connection to Simon and Garfunkel's song 'Scarborough Fair'. Later, I cook some reduced Marks & Spencer salmon with the thyme and some organic olive oil a friend brought me from Italy. This friend has shares in an olive grove and works in a bookshop that is owned by a close relation of Silvio Berlusconi. During the preparation and consumption of this meal, I recognize my cosmopolitanism and briefly regret I can't speak another language. Last time the Daughter stayed she was playing a DJ set at The Coronet, Elephant and Castle. She cooked me a meal using every pot and pan in the kitchen and I was easy with that. I think she Instagrammed the dish.

DOWN TO THE BEACH,
'TIME BOMB' AND PARAFFIN

THE CROWN AND Sceptre, I think I was really happy at that pub, maybe it's because most of my memories only feature myself. In the opening scenes of the 1987 Spielberg film *Empire of the Sun*, based on J.G. Ballard's semi-autobiographical novel, we see Ballard as a young boy on his bicycle, racing around the Japanese-invaded and brutalised Singapore. The luxury of youth: oblivious to the danger, relishing a sense of freedom within the unfolding chaos. When we moved into The Crown, I was out and about from the start. I only remember being introduced to one person, Johnny the heavyweight ex-boxer, who was a friend of my dad's. Johnny worked in a shopfitters round the back of the pub and I would watch him making plywood pistols for me on a huge circular saw. He had a strong Devon accent and was a tough guy. Ever since that time I've loved the smell of sawdust. Several boxers visited or stayed with us, Sammy Abbey from Ghana, Howard Winston from Wales, Commonwealth Games Gold Medallist and the ex-world heavyweight champion Len Harvey, a Cornishman by birth.

Off the main street I used to visit a long, narrow art gallery run by a woman who wore Breton fisherman tops. I'd go there quite a lot – it always smelt of paint and there was an abundance of blue and yellow seaside scenes, ropes and lobster pot props. On the main drag there was a newsagent who sold stink bombs and a sweet shop. The lady who owned the sweet shop had a clubfoot, as did the local cobbler – his shop smelling of leather and glue. He would sharpen our scout knives for free, but we had to give him a coin – a superstition. The second-hand/antique shop with arrow heads and swastika armbands was run by a miserable mother and son. It had a weird vibe – I don't remember either of them as friendly, but I was probably a nuisance asking questions and touching things. Down to the beach, down to the beach – no fear, running, swimming, climbing, chasing. I must have learnt how to swim in the school pool but I loved the sea, diving in from a Victorian construction known as 'The Gentlemen's Bathing Place'. Slipping through cracks in old quarries to big caverns, to the Giants Armchair, looking for treasure and feeding our fantasies. Studying girlie magazines discovered in the woods, carving our initials in trees and discussing a nudist beach that no one had ever visited. Attaching our fantasies to tales of engines so ferocious that they had to be turned over by explosive charges. The *Shooting Star*, a sleek, fast ex-motor torpedo boat from the Second World War. The cigarette boats, the same as the *Shooting Star*, skimming the waves on lakes between Switzerland and Italy, full of contraband, piloted by Lee Marvin or Oliver Reed outrunning the customs cutters, the love interest being Raquel Welch. The war was still active in conversation, artefacts and behaviour. The steps, railings, even parts of the beach are all gone now, the sea turned red with Devon sandstone, coastal erosion. The blue and white porcelain letters naming roads and places, sometimes with a pointing finger, remain cemented onto the locally quarried granite walls in St

Marychurch.

We lived in another pub, The Albert Inn, a small establishment sometimes referred to as 'the little house'. It was just one bar in what would have been two houses knocked together. Mum hated this place, partly due to the smell of rough cider. The Britvic fruit juices were delivered in what looked like ammunition boxes – DJs used these for their 45s. Ted, the guy who serviced the one-armed bandit, drove a baby blue mini van and always gave me half a crown. He committed suicide. This was the first time I had ever heard this term used. We had a brown drop-down bureau that squeaked when opened. I scratched some letters on the front – I don't remember what those letters were or why I did it but I would have got a hiding. Next door was a factory that made Devon Violets perfume. I would use the thrown-out cardboard boxes to make submarines in the long narrow back garden, but I never made friends with anyone who worked there. I don't ever recall friends coming home with me either, apart from the privately educated Philip. He was a white South African whose parents owned the newsagents where I had my weekly subscription to the comic *Buster*, featuring Nutty Slack, The Gentle Grappler. I had also made friends with another boy from South Africa, Anthony, who lived in a big house – big enough to tuck away in the grounds an Austin A30 he'd bought from the gardener for five shillings. I think Anthony became a vicar.

My connection to these boys was stamp collecting. The African stamps were so vibrant and colourful compared to images of Winston Churchill, Lowry paintings, military aircraft and castles. Philip and I would regularly go to the beach together, but on one particular day he had committed some disciplinary infraction at home. The result was that we had to go to the beach separately. It was bizarre seeing each other and not talking but those were the rules.

I have a photograph of my dad holding my daughter's hand on Meadfoot beach in Torquay. He's using a walking stick; he has lost weight and his trousers are belted too tight. He looks vulnerable. This was the last time he was to stand on this beach. I've looked at this image and wondered: Do we have any idea when it's the last time, any clue? With Philip that day at the beach I'm sure that was one of the last times I stuck to the rules. Staying with a friend in an upside-down house in Blagdon village near Bristol, I was given a bundle of letters for bedtime reading after a steak meal and a viewing of the black and white film *The Maltese Falcon* starring Humphrey Bogart. Her great grandfather had written these letters in the trenches of France during the First World War. His last letter before he was killed thanked the family for cigarettes, cake and socks. There was no clue, just no more letters.

For a while I had a Labrador collie cross named Cindy, given to me by a local. I came home from school one day and when I knocked on the door there was no sound of barking. Cindy was gone. Later Mum and Dad took me to the Colony cinema to see *The Sand Pebbles* starring Steve McQueen. In my memory we walked through a dark and closed restaurant to the cinema seats. Of course, this wasn't the reality, yet I remember it all so well. I was left with the legacy of a hopeless situation regarding the storyline of the film, involving someone being shot and falling off a roof. It was all a thoroughly depressing episode.

We moved again. Apparently, Mum kept the books and it was a case of get out now or go bankrupt. We found ourselves living in a flat with a row of lock-up garages opposite. The butcher located on the corner would throw cows' heads out the back and I would find pigs' trotters and chase the girls at school. My brother and I had to share a double bed made up with sheets and blankets, a candlewick bedspread over the top. We'd partition our bed with a hard, long, old-fashioned bolster: I'm sure I recall little bits of charcoal in it. Paraffin heaters were common during this time and I learnt about lighting wicks, and never leaving anything on top of these contraptions made of tin, chrome, and mesh. I was also introduced to the smell of no-nonsense hardware stores and their brown-coated attendants. I recall this period as bleak and cold. At one point, I had cardboard in my shoes. Everything had changed; Mum was doing some secretarial work and Dad was working as a salesman driving about in big, old, black cars borrowed from a dealer whose family owned a dog track. Some of these cars had questionable tax discs that led to the police coming around and having a quiet word. Sometimes, I'd go out with Dad and it felt like old times in London.

At this time Dad's sales involved coal. There was a dock strike that meant coal was not being unloaded from the ships. The deal was you could buy the coal, but you had to unload it yourself and that was how Dad was making his money. I learnt of a coal called anthracite and watched *Jason and the Argonauts* on a colour television in a house in Filton Avenue, Bristol, that belonged to an old boxing pal of Dad's – 'Honest' Joe Pring, who was now a coal merchant. I travelled around quite a bit with Dad during this time and in the car he had an ugly, claret, oblong radio. It had a long brass handle along the top, ran on big bullet-shaped batteries, and was tuned only to medium and long wave. It sat on the back-window parcel shelf for reception reasons and was tuned to Radio Two, the Jimmy Young show. Raymondo, Jimmy's talking chipmunk (the sped-up voice of production assistant Ray Harvey), would ask, "What's the recipe today, Jim?" I didn't want to remember the recipes, all I wanted was Radio One but that was too racy for Dad. There were the books bought from garages: *The Lonely Sea and Sky* by Sir Francis Chichester, an adventurous read of flight and sail, purchased from a petrol station on the Newton Road near Torquay. Another book that I thought was rather lowering the tone was a Batman and Robin story, obtained from a Jet garage near Paignton. The book was thinner with a brightly-coloured cover.

All of a sudden, we're going to New York for Christmas. The Anglo-American Family's Association was an organization that chartered aircraft for people who had relations in the States. We flew Pan Am – I was given a carry-on bag that I treasured for years and was excited to see the Pan Am building lit up with a cross for Christmas in New York. I was taken onto the flight deck of the Boeing 707, possibly because there weren't many children of my age on the flight or maybe it was to keep me quiet. Customs were rude at Kennedy. Nothing changes. I think Mum gave them a run for their money. We stayed with Dad's sister Edna, her husband Brian, and my cousins Heather and John, in Pleasantville, where the *Reader's Digest* was published. I had my new wellington boots to wear in the snow, the boots Mum had been questioned about at the airport. Dad had taken a dartboard over for Brian. Their house had a basement, a settee, and a colour television to watch the Green Bay Packers playing ice hockey. I fashioned a racing car out of balsa wood and entered it in the local Boy Scouts' model car race. Weeks after we'd arrived home, Auntie Edna wrote and told me it had won, but I never received my prize and for years I felt resentful. I visited the fire station with huge red trucks and became a fan of large fridges and ice-cream sandwiches. Uncle Brian gave me a baseball. I have a vague recollection of wearing an American football helmet.

So that Dad and I could get the bus to New York proper, Uncle Brian dropped us at White Plains. I watched the snow ploughs hit the road and sparks fly as they shoved the slush to the sidewalk. We went on a tour of Chinatown, with its dirty green-tinged tanks of living sea creatures in restaurant windows. I complained about a crust over the baked beans in an automat, the type of restaurant where the money is put in a vending machine and you select the food. The woman serving shouted at me, "What's wrong with the beans?"

Looking back, this trip was mostly a sequence of Burroughsian cut-ups with nothing connecting and no beginning, middle, or end. Why didn't we go to Jack Dempsey's restaurant in the Brill Building and have photographic evidence, a tale to tell? But I do remember the booty brought back over the pond, including a big, black, plastic ball with a red fuse called 'Time Bomb'. Instead of musical chairs, this would be wound up and passed round. Whoever was holding it when it went bang was blown up. Plus, there were walkie-talkies and an airline pilot captain's hat.

Of course, there would have been the classroom talk when I got back, the show and tell, everyone getting an insight into my family, like my perception of Northern nosiness masquerading as friendliness. All my confused, conflicting kid-thoughts relating to an epic holiday and then coming home to a flat and sharing a bed with my brother. People not wishing Dad well, seeing him as flash – the homecoming King with his pub and London ways, losing it and swanning off to America. Many of his old school friends had never been anywhere or achieved anything and didn't want to see anyone succeed. The type of men whose wives wished they would shut up.

Relating to this, many years later I'm drinking in a bar with Nigel, whom I would describe as a shadow drinker, the ones that line the wall seats in a pub, the type you acknowledge but then get back to the business in hand. I did time with him once and for his own safety locked him in his cell as some inmates wanted to beat him up for stealing a jar of Robertson's strawberry jam from a prisoner on rule 43 – a sex offender. My argument being that as Nigel was so scrawny, it was bullying to attack him. No one had a go at me.

This particular day he had my attention. He asked me, "So, considering all this stuff you've done, why haven't you got any money?" I felt angry towards him, but worse was the shame. I can even remember the name of the pub where this happened, The Klondike – it doesn't exist anymore.

I have other memories around this pub, selling a Ford Cortina and £40 worth of speed hidden up a nearby alley. The cut-ups again: no real beginning, middle, or end. I can almost hear, through the shout of last orders and the bell ringing, Bill Burroughs wheezing, "Gerry, wait for the set-up man…" And if you've ever read *Junkie*, you'll know the set-up man never arrives.

I don't think I was ever innocent. Nothing ever came as a shocking surprise. I'd had peculiar disappointments that had made me more resilient. One I never forgot was talking to a workman while my mum was in hospital. I was staying with a family in the fishing town of Brixham. I can imagine myself as talkative, trusting, a bit overactive. I told him my granddad had been in a Japanese prisoner of war camp and gave him his name and where he was from. He led me along telling me he knew him. I'd never met my granddad and I was really excited about it. Then, the next day he told me he didn't know him and it wasn't true. I was just quiet and upset but this really affected me. It served as an introduction to the complexity of human emotion.

My friendship with Philip from the newsagents receded at this point and I started knocking about with some lads I went to school with. Behind the row of lock-up garages across the road from the flat was a large golf course and stories of massive tips for caddying circulated like fishing tales of 'the one that got away'. I'd sometimes go and do a bit of putting but it wasn't my game, especially after I got hit on the nose with a club, standing too close. I don't think my nose ever bled afterwards. I was always more of a doorstep opportunist, honing my skills from the days of scouting Bob a Job – mostly a lone operator.

Small towns and moving about. The rateable value of your house – pre-council tax and the view, the social barometer of location, location. *Now after school you come home to 47 Warbro Road, it's on the road by the Walls Ice Cream factory near the traffic lights.* Going to school from one address and going home to a new one – with new smells. It was one of those cusping addresses, it could be Plainmoor, near the Torquay United football ground, or for the purpose of bed and breakfast adverts in Daltons Weekly it could be Babbacombe. Both addresses are correct. The house belongs to my parents, they've bought it – the mystery deepens and is never quite answered. This house was rather like an old coat, a coat you want, but it doesn't quite fit and there are bus tickets in the pockets to places you can't pronounce. All the furniture and effects of the previous owner were still in place, down to the cutlery in the drawers. I remember a black beret with a leather sweatband on a hook in what would have been an outside toilet if it were not for the glass conservatory roof. I created a history around that beret involving Field Marshal Montgomery and tank battles in the Libyan Desert, always the Libyan Desert.

This house was never in the image of ourselves. Most of my parents' furniture from their early married days had been sold, as we didn't have the space at The Albert or storage later on. The radiogram survived, along with the backlit cocktail cabinet-cum-sideboard and the bureau with the scratched initials. The only significant item, which lived in the cocktail cabinet, was Dad's bulky brown scrapbook – it now resides in the archive of Torquay museum – usually taken out for the benefit of front room drinkers.

It had three bedrooms, a garden that Dad would concrete over, front room and a parlour, plus a kitchen. We were still using the paraffin heaters though, going to the self-service machine outside the garage down the road. Two bob or 10 pence pieces, filling the can with the funny nozzle with Esso Blue or Pink paraffin. The grass died under the old furniture thrown out into the garden; a wardrobe on its back became a ship until it was hauled away to the tip. I don't remember anything particularly good coming out of this address, and a lot of bad decisions were made there. The next-door house, the Vinton's, had a huge coffin shed out the back – Mrs. Vinton's husband had been an undertaker. The teacher daughter would sunbathe in a bikini – she was called Launa, I don't know what she taught.

The real story was under the stairs, the long khaki-coloured canvas two-handled zip-up kitbag. In the bag were the long-tongued, black leather-soled boxing boots with faded, white laces, some Everlast gold monogrammed shorts, and a red, silk dressing gown with 'Paul King, Torquay' embroidered in gold lettering on the back. There was also a blue concertina toolbox with an assortment of tools: pipe cutter with hair-lipped snouts, blunt and long-nosed pliers, coiled solder, black cloth insulation tape, and small screws pillowed in flux. Representing my mum was a light blue Olivetti travelling typewriter with small white quick release square buttons either side of the handle.

LSD, RIMSKY KORSAKOV
AND SINNET'S LOCKER

THERE WERE CHRISTIANS living further along the road, and I stole money from various After Eight box shaped collection boxes scattered around their house. I was to razor in (on a wheeled trolley in their front room) half of my first ever tab of pink microdot LSD. I would drop the tab and start tripping in a grey Morris 1000 – the particular gearbox whine associated with this car to be forever fixed in my memory. We'd visit the Christians' daughter, who had a flat overlooking a bowling green near Paignton seafront. I remember peeling an orange on the kitchen floor and thinking about how the orange was in pieces because of me. Maybe she gave me the orange on purpose as vitamin C was known to lessen a trip. Her name was Rose, it was unrequited love, a bit of a crush. Sometime previously, my mum had challenged me about stealing. She asked me to swear on the Bible that I hadn't stolen some item or other. I swore on the Bible and nothing happened, so I kept on stealing. I would steal to buy things that made me feel better. I acquired an unusual habit, bearing in mind I was not Catholic, of repeating 'God forgive' three times if I used the word 'fuck'. At some point, this chanting did stop but certainly not the swearing. I'd try to do good things, redeemable acts like sending a blanket to Bangladesh after seeing the ex-Beatle George Harrison's film *Concert for Bangladesh*. I sewed my initials into the blanket and handed it over to the Christians up the road.

I had a girlfriend, Sheila Penny, and later another girlfriend, Penny Bell. A lot of kissing was involved with both of them. Sheila had dark, curly, short hair. She was a year older than me and rather serious; I found this trait attractive, lending her some mystery. I once sent her a letter with a mint 1947 stamp on it. Penny was a strawberry blonde, grammar school girl, two years older than me and extremely adventurous, very much an open book. Her brother had acted as her emissary, contacting me after Penny had seen me walking past her mother's nursing home, carrying a number of LPs including Hawkwind's *Master of the Universe*. Her mother was matron of a large council-run care home, situated behind my local café where I used to scoff cheese on toast with beans and poached egg. Penny's brother went to the same school as me and said his sister would like to meet me. The café was a meeting point and one of the regulars was a guy called Andy whose summer gig was working the fairground.

Every season Andy worked on the Anderton and Rowlands Fun Fair when it came to Torquay, setting up on Walls Hill, a large, open common area near the Babbacombe Theatre. I knew this fair well as Dad had once boxed on their booth and every time they came to Torquay he'd take bottles of Guinness down to Ester McKeowen who was on the booth door. Andy sported a greasy, swept-back rockabilly hairstyle and wore a battered leather jacket with a BSA logo on the back, oily, blue jeans with big turn-ups and German paratrooper boots. The snub-nosed Scammell lorries ran thick black power cables from their heavy-duty whirring generators to the various rides contributing to this industrial-entertainment complex. The screaming sirens, whooping and wailing, signalled the end of the ride and the guy in the booth spieled up the next Waltzer adventure as Andy would lift the chrome safety bars. Slowing to a stop, the punters got out and the new intake ran up the steps and into the rounded-back cars. Andy collected the dough, put the bars down, and slowly the platform started moving. 'All Right Now' by Free was banging out over the chain-suspended big, black boxy speakers, the bassline almost synchronizing with the rise and fall of the platform. Picking up speed, the cars would start spinning round and round, abruptly whipping back in the opposite direction. Screams, shouts, and laughter – the simplicity of the moment. Andy floated over the platform flirting and flashy, combing his hair one-handed while holding the back of a Waltzer. The fabulously painted fairground attractions provided the props and backdrop for everyone to play out their parts, perfect the performance. The pole-dancing boys rode the spark-raining dodgems, leaning into the cars with the giggling girls – counting the coins into one hand, tipping the change over and palming 10 pence or two bob. *You fuck with one of us –you fuck with all of us.* Andy would light a cigarette and promenade in the opposite direction to the ride, moving around the undulating worn wooden Waltzer platform, staying cool and looking mean. In this instant, he was the king of all he surveyed.

During the winter months, Andy's stage was disassembled, packed up, and put on the back of a Scammell or an AEC to be stored in a showman's yard in Old Market, Bristol. I'd see Andy around town; he was always on his own. I never knew where he lived, or anything about him really. I'd see him in the local café playing the pinball machine, one leg lifting off the floor when he got aggressive on the flippers. He looked a tough guy, but intrinsically I knew he wasn't a nasty piece of work – he'd always nod, acknowledging me, just a kid, throwing me a bone of acceptance. I found out things and made connections, from the Warhol Super-Stars celebrated in Lou Reed's 'Walk on the Wild Side', and Ian Dury in the late 1970s with a withered leg, wonderful music hall lyrics and a menacing presence. Andy had a clubfoot but when he was on that Waltzer you'd never know it – he was a king without a crown. Words I read and understood but couldn't properly pronounce – it took Ian Dury to spell it out as to why Andy had a clubfoot and the local cobbler and the woman who ran the sweet shop. It was polio. I don't think Andy ever had a motorbike.

Penny was to come around to my house with her brother to listen to music and her brother was sent home – early. One night we both dropped acid and after unsuccessfully trying to have sex through a fit of giggles, decided to go into town down to the harbour. We were wearing identical white, fleecy zip-up hoodies my grandmother had sent from the States. Her parcels would arrive at least twice a year and contain really unusual clothes by UK standards. Sometimes the clothes would conceal a box of King Edward's cigars for Dad. He was dressed like Robert DeNiro in *Casino* during most of the 1970s and I was known at school as Pyjama Boy for my colourful sports kit. Penny and I were tripping, slightly paranoid, slinking down all the back alleyways with our hoods up trying to be inconspicuous and totally failing. I can still imagine the scenarios of 'who will go into the newsagents for a packet of cigarettes', the whispered debates and trade-offs on the pavement, "You go in, he doesn't know you – I had a paper round here". Avoiding eye contact and the dread of a neighbour or family friend greeting us as we navigated a whole new adventure. People usually took on the features of animals when I was tripping – horses, wolves or cats. Jumble sales were a brilliant source of entertainment after the initial fear subsided. Another momentary delight was to make a purchase from the hatched-off sales at the pub and look through at the old regulars in the snug bar. The smoking crones, supping their Mackeson stout like Minnie Caldwell and Ena Sharples of *Coronation Street*, and Albert Tatlock in his mac and thick, black-rimmed glasses. A generation that had marvelled at State Pensions, foreign holidays and the NHS, now having to contend with giggling youths, their pupils like saucers, popping their heads through the hatch for a gander. It is possible my reputation as the 'outsider', the weird kid, was engendered through school friends' horse-headed mothers, their patterned head scarves pulled tight over their manes, gossiping to each other in the butchers, "I saw that Paul King's boy the other day in the jumble – just stands there staring and giggling – he might be a bit simple".

And the response possibly something along the lines of, "Well, his father was a boxer – probably too many punches to the head".

Sometime around here was my jumping-off point. Not gateway drugs as I always wanted to go further into what I suppose was a subculture, something more exotic – the other. It was different and exciting, the clothes, the colours, the smells, the girls and the music. *International Times* posters bought from the Tangerine Fuzz boutique along with concert tickets for the Town Hall to see Hawkwind and Mott the Hoople. A wet Afghan coat and patchouli oil; green satin loons; a black, embroidered kaftan; desert boots; and a dirty, beige canvas gas-mask bag with my school books in. Playing truant and going to a bedsit in Ellacombe Church Road where some hippy friends lived – the drug squad busting the place, leather jackets, moustaches, and Brut aftershave. I hid in the wardrobe only to be discovered and when asked what I was doing there, I said, "My homework". Thankfully, they thought this was amusing. The police searched me and one of the hippies said that I was a family friend and I'd brought an LP back.

An old pal reminded me on Facebook recently that I'd turned up at school assembly one morning wearing a cloak fashioned out of a bed sheet with the words 'Hendrix is God' written on the back. I was sent home to change and came back wearing a top hat and tails. Those were the days you could find the most incredible outfits in charity shops, from WWII American flak jackets to Japanese embroidered waistcoats. I remember paying 50p for a coat with tails. Oxfam was always expensive compared to the Salvation Army.

During the miners' strike, when all the power was out, I remember climbing up a metal fire escape into a cold winter let – it was all very *Midnight Cowboy* on a low cal tenement level. We'd huddle around candles and battery radios – *this is Radio Luxembourg on 208 metres* – with adverts for the fragrance of 'Aqua Manda' by Goya and 'Dateline, 23 Abingdon Road, London'. I particularly remember Dateline, as Penny's mother met a suitor through this agency.

At first, I got on well with Penny's mother; she was the ex-wife of an army dentist and had something of the Billie Whitelaw about her. However, Penny was to write a letter to her friend in Birmingham telling of our midnight raids on the outside storeroom of a local off-licence. Her mother found the letter and, as a consequence, I was *persona non grata* for about five years afterwards. I was excluded again when I drove Dad's Jag all over the lawn of the nursing home dropping Penny back one night. Penny bought me Python Lee Jackson's 'In a Broken Dream' for my 15th birthday. We parted soon after and I then went out with Susan, who ironed her hair and could sit on it.

I had a pal called Jimmy whose parents owned a fancy goods shop and we would trip together on a regular basis. One particular weekend, I couldn't get hold of him and wasn't sure if he had scored the acid. I phoned his parents and they told me he was at the ABC cinema at Castle Circus. I called the cinema, pretending to be either his mum or dad, gave them my phone number and asked them to contact him as there was an emergency at home. The announcement went up on the screen and we sorted our trip out. Some years down the line, Penny and Jimmy entered into a sort of mutually destructive Keith Richard and Anita Pallenberg relationship. A terrible car crash in the late 70s left both of them sustaining serious head injuries. Jimmy never fully recovered. Penny emigrated to Australia in the mid 80s and married an abusive chef.

I had been a member of the army cadets and applied their night manoeuvres training I had learnt at Anzio camp, Leek, Staffordshire, to stealing from motors in hotel car parks. I would open the car doors, turn the interior lights off and stand stock still with my mouth open listening for any movement. In those days it was the sound of blood rushing around my head – now it is tinnitus and air conditioning. There were episodes that, at the time, I would have found funny. One hot summer night with a torch under my chin, I opened a metal-framed Crittall ground floor window of the Sun Ray Hotel and shouted, "Rimsky Korsakov!", before throwing talcum powder over the people in the bed.

The phrase was the strap-line for a soft drink made by Cresta. The animated advert was popular at this time, featuring a polar bear with sunglasses on. The bear would take a sip of the drink and shout, "Rimsky Korsakov! It's frothy, man". Crasher, a pal from Plymouth, had the bear sporting a huge erection tattooed on his arm. His party trick was to expose himself, displaying a red rose with 'Bless You' inked around his tackle.

I loved the night. I was a fast runner and felt invincible as I knew every lane and short cut. Taunton Natural Dry cider played a significant part, as opposed to the sweet Autumn Gold, along with Benzedrex inhalers. My cassette collection was entirely made up of other people's musical tastes; Neil Young and Carole King were a welcome introduction from an insecure MG sports car. These actions do taint my memories though, defiling my introduction to music and styles I've come to cherish – almost a Duchampian stolen collection of ready-made culture. It was amazing what people would leave in cars. One night, myself and John of the London scouts' trip, took a large sum of money in mixed silver and notes out of a car. It belonged to someone who emptied amusement machines. Later, when we got into a taxi and the suspension went down slightly, I told the driver it was books for my college-catering course. John and I thoroughly enjoyed acid, usually laughing manically throughout the night while listening to 'Radar Love' by the Dutch band Golden Earring, as well as David Bowie's 'The Man Who Sold the World'. At John's house, I had been known to mow the sloping lawn on a boring Sunday wearing one of his mum's dresses with the stereo speakers on a window ledge belting out *Live Johnny Winter And*.

John's mum, Phyllis, with her flaming red hair, plain Players cigarettes, and gold sovereign ring, found my antics hilarious and supported this attention-seeking self-expression. We always felt Sundays needed kicking up a gear, those lazy afternoons of black and white films and an ice cream van if you were lucky, pubs closing at 2pm and not opening until 7pm. Sunday: the day of amorous pursuits with a girl called Catherine and her sister after a cider house visit. Catherine was my age and her sister, who was in control and didn't say much, a little older. Their brother was to do time for murder. That Johnny Winter album was special to me, especially as I'd sneaked into the staff room at school and removed it from Mr Sinnet's locker. I made sure he saw me swanning past his glass-walled classroom with the album under my arm. Some weeks previously I'd had to leave his class early and left my Johnny Winter album on my desk. When I asked him if he'd seen it, he told me he hadn't. The music caught the spirit of my attitude, especially Winter's version of 'Jumping Jack Flash'. John's house was like a second home; it was on a council estate that had a reputation, but I never felt threatened.

I realized my antics couldn't continue, but, as I incrementally discovered, the reality was never as bad as my own imagination or the violence worse than what I had seen or had touched my family. The truanting, the stealing, the drinking and taking drugs, the sex with girlfriends – what would I do if I didn't do all this? I had some idea of what I should be doing but I didn't have the staying power. I was easily distracted and tempted. Even at this age, I had a *mañana* attitude, and all the threats and warnings never lived up to my expectations. I didn't believe how the story could end; familial precedence didn't bode well either, with certainly no stories of fabulous achievements. Everything seemed to be struggle and blame, one way or the other.

The summer of 1973. Snatching the cashbox out of a Chinese restaurant with John, we were pursued by two off-duty coppers. Dad collected me from the police station. Mum was away in London. At 3:00 a.m., Dad came home from the club, woke me up and gave me a hiding.

Months after this drama, there were occasions during the early hours when Jimmy and I would be tripping off our boxes in my room quietly listening to music like *On the Threshold of a Dream* by the Moody Blues when we'd hear the closing clicking Yale and rattly glass of Dad coming in the front door, his advance through the house given away by creaking floorboards. *Who's afraid of the big bad wolf?* Frequently half-cut on the largess of the club punters, he would mutter to himself and we would pray he wouldn't come into the bedroom. We'd listen to him horse-pissing in the toilet and the potential legacy of nightclubbing violence was almost tangible, seeping like a mist under the door. *Ooh, I'm delicate, don't hit me.* The cord pull would click on and off in the bathroom always louder at night and the fanlight flashed its signal above my bedroom door. Eventually, all would settle.

FULLAFORD HOUSE

I RAN AWAY from home after the 3:00 a.m. violence, living at various large crumbling Victorian houses awaiting demolition, set in their own grounds in beautiful areas of Torquay, their gardens home to gangly fig trees. Sometimes I would stay at John's house and the law would come around half-heartedly looking for me. I wasn't unhappy – I had girlfriends, pals I knocked about with, and I could look after myself. I was always working, usually in local hotels, and could support myself. The school summer holidays were coming to an end and I knew if I didn't go back to school I'd be in more trouble. I turned up as normal but during my first day back I was called into the headmaster's office where a policeman was waiting. I was taken over to Paignton police station where a civilian forensics man, who drove a wooden-panelled Morris 1000 estate, asked me if I'd broken in to anywhere and told me that if I had, they would find out because they had my fingerprints. I explained I worked and lived in abandoned houses, making sure I kept John's mum, Phyllis, out of the frame. They seemed quite impressed with this and I don't recall them being mean to me. Later that day, I was taken to Buckfastleigh.

September 1973, Fullaford House, Buckfastleigh, Devon: I was placed in the care of the local authority. This institution doesn't exist now; an upmarket housing estate of semi- and detached housing has been built on the site. One of the housemasters of this institution was to be imprisoned for 17 years in 2000 for historical sexual abuse offences committed before he worked at the House. I was fortunate he didn't try to abuse me, but he did goad a big lump of a farm boy from Barnstaple into fighting me in a rough and ready gym hut. This was one of those times when I realized I had the ability to talk my way out of a threatening situation. Somehow, I managed to spin it so that we both ended up asking this bastard what he was playing at. A visit from my dad one Saturday afternoon, half-cut, leery and sentimental, warned this guy off when he tried to question him about taking me out. We'd drive around in the Corsair, Cat Stevens playing 'Wild World' on an eight-track the old man bought from someone when he was on the door of Barons, a Plymouth nightclub. Stopping in a café for awkward tea and cakes, I was relieved when I was back on my own. I gained some form of protection from these visits but no comfort as Dad was mixed up with another woman and he was clearly distracted. His guard was down with me, but I was wary.

Dad only ever visited once with Mum at Fullaford. The housemaster decided I was to go to school every day in Torquay to study for my GCSEs – it was a round trip of 34 miles. I would get a taxi from Buckfastleigh together with two other kids who attended a school for children with learning difficulties in Torquay. The taxi would take us as far as Totnes, dropping us outside a comprehensive school, King Edward VI, now a Community College, where we'd pick up a minibus for the rest of the daily journey. One morning the minibus didn't turn up. We were outside the school waiting and it became evident it wasn't coming. I recognized that the kids I was with were getting anxious, as up to this point there had been a routine and we'd never deviated from it. I told them to come with me and thankfully they followed me into the school without any fuss. We somehow found ourselves in the art room, the teacher sat them down with paper and crayons and everything was alright. It wasn't an English, maths, or woodwork class – it was an art class. That stayed with me.

Eventually, I arrived in Torquay and went to see my mum, who was working in a cake shop near my school. I told her what had happened, but she didn't even give me a free cake. I remember that. No doubt she was having a hard time at home, just her and my brother Ian, and she was probably having to work in that shop because Dad was being tight with money. A free cake might have compromised her, but I didn't think of that then.

It was strange going back into the family home to get some of my stuff (like my *The Velvet Underground & Nico* and Rolling Stones' LPs) from what had been my bedroom, and then having to return to Buckfastleigh. I gave my copy of *Live at Max's Kansas City* by The Velvet Underground, which I'd bought from a record shop in Soho on a London excursion, to a lad I knocked about with for a while. I met him one weekend when we both came home on leave from Fullaford. He had arranged to see a man in some woods near Gasworks Beach, Paignton. The man pulled up in a brown Morris Marina; I scratched the number plate of his car in the instep of my leather Russell and Bromley shoes. He went into the woods to exchange sex for money, asking me if I wanted to do it. I said no. I endeavoured to present a front of coolness, when in fact I was rather shocked. He seemed quite blasé about the whole thing and it transpired this was a regular arrangement. Even though I obtained my money predominately by theft, I judged him. I considered myself lucky that I didn't have to do what he did for money and I decided not to hang about with him after that. It just wasn't my scene.

Some nights at Fullaford I would sneak out the drop-down basement window in the snooker room and go down to the off-sales at the pub and buy a bottle of cider, always on my own. It was a comfort and I felt better looking at life through a filter. There were other times when tea was over and the thought of boys in front of a television and then up to a dormitory bed just wasn't enough. I had options, not sanctioned, but I had a girlfriend and a pal I could get up to no good with – I'd just think 'fuck it' and go. I had a network outside the house but for some of the others this was it. If they were lucky, they'd be able to ride their bicycle to the council apprenticeship when the time came, but scenarios like that filled me with dread. I was always polite to the staff, making sure I had my cigarettes and whatever money I'd stashed. Matches in one pocket, cigarettes in the other – 50 pence pieces and pound notes. It was so simple then, so few possessions.

Once I'd made my mind up, without any discussion, I would jump out of the drop-down snooker room window into the late autumn dusk, feeling the seduction of this snatched moment. That sense of recklessness; running down the grassy slope, slipping and sliding, past the walled garden, through a field to a farmer's gate, vaulting over and out to the lane, down to the A38. *It'll be alright, I'll get out of this later.* I knew I would, as if I had lives to use up. There was one particular night when I'd hitched a lift in a Ford Anglia, the driver picking me up just before a bend, and as we went around, I saw a police car sitting back from the road. This driver was going to work at Centrax in Newton Abbot, a factory that then made aircraft blades for the engines of Concorde. He was using a battery-operated shaver – I thought that was rather cool. I'd then get another lift from Newton Abbot to Torquay and make straight for John's house, arriving before closing time. Phyllis' boyfriend Chris would be there. He was a big guy with long, unruly, receding hair, and a broken pug-nose. He'd fought in the army – Borneo was mentioned. I once hid in a bed with him when the police came looking for me, knowing they wouldn't ask him to get out. Phyllis would greet me with a hug and lipstick kiss on the cheek, "What the bloody hell are you up to?" I felt safe, like I was home in that front room of smoke, booze, and Dick Emery on the television. Phyllis' cat was a Siamese called Thomas with large balls. I've never really been a cat man, but Thomas was different. Eventually, I would have to go back to the care home; usually an arrangement was made with my social worker. Not quite a Checkpoint Charlie, Berlin defector moment, but in my full-length leather coat, I would have certainly embellished the boring reality.

I started a three-page magazine at Fullaford – I wish I had a copy now. I somehow managed to get the smokers' aged over 16 legal access to an agreed number of cigarettes per day. I said that secretly smoking in the basement near the oil boiler was dangerous and, as the local authority was legally our parents, they should give us permission, and so they did. I was left to my own devices for years; I had to look out for myself and I somehow got through these baby step institutional environments, looking for wardrobes to Narnia and building cardboard submarines wherever I went. I'm guessing Dad's advice would have been along the lines of, "Keep your head down and don't let anyone take liberties". Bullying was never an issue – I intrinsically knew how to play people. The secret was the integrity – they had to believe me. There would have been a few smacks in the chops but nothing that endured. I made friends with Richard LePage, a young ginger-haired housemaster. He eventually left the job and I would occasionally stay with him and his girlfriend in a nearby cottage. They brewed fizzy beetroot wine, which I really enjoyed. I remember the cook at Fullaford House; she was a squat, round, kind-hearted Devonian woman, who – I imagine – would have been a marvellous grandmother. She made me a big bowl of porridge every morning when I had to go to school in Torquay. Rather than disappoint her, I would sometimes pour the porridge down the toilet.

I would always compare my situation to those who were in dire circumstances and tell myself it wasn't that bad. But throughout all those days and nights of running wild, I must have realized this is not how people behave, this is not what kids do at my age. Some years previously, I threw a stone at the window of a neighbour's house. I think it was a Sunday night; I could see a family in warm, subdued light watching TV, and I threw that stone through their window, waiting just long enough to witness the ensuing shock. Mum had once asked the Christians I had stolen from if I could stay with them for a few days while she went to London to be with her ailing father. They told her it wasn't possible. I realized if there was any opportunity of getting me to stay with other people it happened. When I was a kid it was all an adventure, not a *Guardian* article or an excuse to blame; I really didn't think it was a big deal. I thought most of it was my fault because I was hyperactive and stole things.

MORE THAN A BUNCH OF NAUGHTY KIDS

LATE NOVEMBER I moved from Fullaford, where I had my 16th birthday, to an adolescent unit in Exeter. My hair-ironing girlfriend, Susan, bought me *Ooh La La* by The Faces. I knew I was pushing my luck and, bearing in mind I was always up to no good, I had suspected that the next stop after the children's home would be approved school. Miss Bethell, the Triumph Herald driving social worker, had suggested this unit in Exeter, explaining to me it was where troubled young people were encouraged to talk about their problems. Researching it later, I found this description of the residence: 'The Dryden children's special unit for disturbed adolescents'. I was on another adventure, except this was in the wing of a hospital and the set-up was run by a Druid psychiatrist. I think he was a well-intentioned individual and I never read anything disparaging about him, despite so much abusive malarkey coming to light about institutions during the 1970s. There were girls and boys in this place; I don't remember anyone being dangerous, but we were more than a bunch of naughty kids. When Mum and Dad met the psychiatrist, Mum told me later that he had said to Dad, "Mr King, we're here to talk about Gerry, not you".

I considered myself quite successful in most of my exploits up until this point, but of course it was all based on secrets. I had some nice clothes and an attractive girlfriend with her own cheque book. Realistically, I had experienced much beyond my age – earlier that year I'd walked off with several hundred pounds from a distraction theft. I'd discovered morphine at £2 a bag and started snorting it, was drinking in pubs, going to clubs, and catching the train up to London to buy clothes and records. Quite a few of the people I knocked about with didn't realize how young I was, especially two young nurses I'd go out drinking with and end up crashing together at their place. I'd also worked at an assortment of jobs from seafront fish and chip bars to Indian and Greek restaurants. Abdul Siddique (I liked Siddique) had put a sign in his restaurant window: 'Wanted cleaner and help in kitchen weekends'. At the Curry Royal my duties involved steering a big upright Hoover vacuum cleaner around the restaurant; it had a light that illuminated the underneath of the tables. Then, I'd be in the kitchen. Siddique was meticulous about clean cutlery, insisting on two boiled rinses. I think of Siddique even now when I wash my cutlery. He was a good man to work for and I loved the zany humour of things lost in translation. Many years later, I was doing business with some Bengalis in Glastonbury and I mentioned Siddique. They were really impressed, "You knew Abdul Siddique of the Curry Royal?" Apparently, he was something of a legend in the Bengali community.

As I was to find out, Zoff plaster remover and Lady Esquire shoe cleaner were the recreational drugs of choice in Dryden, and the shampoo was Head and Shoulders. Dad brought his girlfriend to visit and took me into town to a jeweller to get his wedding ring altered to fit me. This was a journey into the weird and on one occasion I drove a tractor through the double doors of a barn, ending up in an observation room, shot up with Largactil. There was regular group therapy. As I remember, we could smoke and there were big freestanding chrome ashtrays placed throughout the room. Somebody nearly always ran out crying and I made a point of not getting involved with any of the girls. What was it all about? Nights spent sitting with male nurses in the office smoking and listening to how they'd put a Lotus engine into a Cortina. I don't remember any schooling but there must have been. We did go into the community helping out at various institutions and services with old people and the homeless. I clearly remember those outings and always thought they were a brilliant idea. I'd been involved in something like this before – at Fullaford we'd go to Moorhaven, a psychiatric hospital outside Plymouth. We would push patients about, taking them into the hall that served as a cinema on a Saturday afternoon. One week we all watched the murder mystery *Klute,* starring Donald Sutherland as a detective and Jane Fonda as a high-class prostitute. Admittedly, I'd seen Ken Russell's *The Devils* and Ralph Bakshi's *Fritz the Cat* when I was 13 at the local ABC, but I thought screening *Klute* in this environment was questionable – the system didn't give a fuck for its charges then and probably gives less now.

We were taken one morning to the Simon Community, a shelter for homeless men. It was a big old house; a crumbling dwelling sharing similar architectural features of the grand houses in Clifton, Bristol. It had been badly converted, I could imagine all the original fixtures had been removed, and it was in need of serious renovation, but like most of the residents, it was on its last legs awaiting demolition, a temporary arrangement.

Coming out of a waffle house on Kings Road in Chelsea with my family early in the 1960s, there was a man sitting on a blanket on the pavement and another man standing beside him. They both looked like tramps. My dad stopped and spoke to them. I noticed he gave them money and I asked him who they were. He explained that the guy sitting on the floor was a former world champion boxer and the man standing with him was his pal, keeping an eye out for him, watching his back. On another occasion, I was with my dad one night when he picked up a hitchhiker, who was on his way to be blessed at St Martin in the Fields near the National Gallery in London, before going out on the road. Some of these men would never have signed on, wouldn't have accepted state handouts, even though they would have been entitled.

Peter Howson, the Scottish artist, paints such subjects; predominantly masculine men with chiselled features virtually hewn out of granite. In particular, *The Noble Dosser,* a man comfortable in his bulky overcoat, shirtless with a kerchief round his neck, fag in his plate-sized hand resting on a riveted bollard, staring defiantly into the future. Howson was an official war artist during the 1990s Bosnian conflict. He would have seen things that one can't forget. The growly East London actor Steven Berkoff commented, "Howson's figures have eyes that see the world clearly, however blind they are to themselves". I've met men like this, men with flattened noses and blunt knuckles, wearing shabby, greasy overcoats. I've witnessed their ranting street theatrics, their drink-soaked histrionics. Some of these guys had experienced the violent abuse of Reading Recall and Preventative Detention, hardcore establishment brutality. A leaking uncontrollable sadness. I noticed these men sober on prison landings with big, scuffed, white, plastic jugs full of tea, ambling along to Alcoholics Anonymous meetings in the chapel. I knew them by name, and they knew me. There were to be instances when I'd see them on the out – sometimes in their pain – we'd recognize each other and, in that moment, there would be a reprieve.

The sleeping arrangements in the Simon community were mattresses on the floor. A man had died the previous night and nobody – for whatever reason or superstition – wanted to remove the mattress. I helped someone drag the mattress out to put it on a fire, and as we did so I discovered the dead man's tobacco tin under his pillow. I handed it over to one of the workers. There was another venue we'd help out in, a lunch centre for old people where we'd serve the food and do the washing up.

I'd really come to dislike Christmas – the enforced joviality, everyone around the table pretending and expected to do a turn. The last Christmas I'd enjoyed was in 1971 at John's flat with his mum and her boyfriend Chris. The flat was above a fruit shop and as a kid it seemed massive. John Kongos' *Tokoloshe Man* always brings this time back to me. I was 14 years old and I was working in the Carlton Club helping the chef in the restaurant, slicing the Melba toast and making up the prawn cocktails. Dad was on the door and I can still conjure up the subdued atmosphere of the club prior to opening, the anticipation of the performance. The predominant colours of the interior were purple and cream. People would enter through glass double doors with brass motif handles and walk up the carpeted stairs past the cloakroom. A feature with fronded plants in a sea of sunken pebbles and stones was placed before the restrooms like a huge, beige, plastic bath. Taking a right turn here you would be in the bar, run by Andy, a bald Greek. I never warmed to him – he was not to be trusted. Directly to the left of the bar was the restaurant, slightly raised with a seating area and a chiller fridge countertop. To the right was the club proper with a small stage area for the drummer, guitarist and electric keyboards behind the dance floor. The exhaust fans would come on for the night, starting above the fryers, the huge trunking running through the kitchen. There would be a last-minute bottling up behind the bar, kerchinging of change going into the tills, waitresses wearing hot pants, and banter with the door staff. The lingering smells of cigarettes and cigars, perfume and aftershave; sophisticated fragrances for a young boy. It was amazing to be part of this adult world – my little secret. Like the battery memory in a mobile phone, when you first get one you give them a good long charge, so the memory retains that charge. Those hours were my battery charging, hardwired into my psyche. I've always been a night owl. The pace and rhythm throughout the night, the resident band, the cabaret spots, comedians, the singers and the songs – 'The Windmills of your Mind' can take me there in a flash. The hours were eight till two in the morning. I'd go home with Dad after he'd dropped the waitresses off; he always waited for them to go in their front doors. Twenty-five pence an hour, one pound, 50p – 30 bob a night.

Going home for Christmas from the Dryden Centre... I shared a bedroom with my brother. We slept in bunk beds with crudely drawn ivy and the words written on one post: 'Is it worth the climb?' relating to when Penny left me late 1972. I think she was my first love and turned me on to the music of Leonard Cohen. She went off with Jerry, a hippy I'd introduced her to. Life lessons, I guess. I consider this time, this particular year and the coming event, my Altamont Speedway moment. Altamont was a free festival that took place in California on 6th December 1969.

The Rolling Stones were the headline act. It is said that much of what happens in America finally finds its way over here. At Altamont the security was organised by some Hell's Angels. Not a bad thing in itself, but the particular chapter that covered the security was drunk, tripping, and out of control. It followed that what was supposed to be another Woodstock of peace and love descended into violence, mayhem, and ultimately murder. While Altamont marked the end of the hippy era, what was to happen at the Carlton Club, Torquay, on the night of 21st December 1973 was a moment when all my juvenile irresponsibility manifested itself into something really dark. Drink, drugs, depression, prison, internecine relationships, the whole 10 yards and it took me two decades to emerge from. I don't blame my later conduct on what happened, but it did sort of raise the bar on extreme behaviour touching my family and how you dealt with it.

Mum woke me up in the early hours, "There's been a shooting at the club".

I asked, "Did they get Dad?"

She replied, "No". I rolled over and went back to sleep. Marty Fenton, a gunman, had walked into the Torquay nightclub where Dad worked with two pistols and shot three people dead. I knew two of these – one was the casino manager Leondros and the other was Austin Webb who managed the Gibbons Hotel on the Strand. I'd worked for Austin Webb briefly during the summer of 1972. Fenton shot a policeman dead on the way to the club; he would have shot my dad but by the time Fenton noticed him, he had run out of bullets. Some months earlier, Fenton had pulled a knife out in the club and I was told Dad had disarmed him, wrapping his tuxedo around his arm and battering him. Somehow Andy the snide Greek barman had spirited the blade away. The shooting scenario was almost a Shakespearian tragedy, an accumulation of events and an example of the complexity of feuds, men, money, violence and warped loyalty. Fenton owned a catering company and had supplied and fitted out the club, but he had started gambling in the casino. Apparently, when he was losing, he'd been told the money could be taken off what he was owed. He lost a lot.

I don't remember where I was for that particular Christmas in 1973. I do know I went back to Exeter, but I'm not sure if any other kids were there. I had a locker with a drop-down flap and in that locker at one point was a tin of cigars – thin Panetelas, the proceeds of a late-night pub visit. A few of us would go out to the local boozers around Exeter. Awful jukebox music marks this period: Suzi Quatro, Leo Sayer, and Showaddywaddy. The year started low-cal; it seemed to permeate everything, especially taste and decisions. I was aware my standards were dropping, almost as if I'd peaked. I recall buying shoes, slightly platformed, with cream crepe soles whereas the previous year I'd bought tasteful two-tone brown leather from Russell and Bromley. Eventually, I just went home to Mum and Dad as they were back together after a break-up. But other people were living in the house as Dad converted the downstairs into a self-contained flat, the idea being the rent would have provided Mum's maintenance. Needless to say, I'd spend most of my time up at John's. That was until he got arrested for stealing from cars, caught by his fingerprints; then off to Borstal with him. We'd had a plan to buy a burger van.

DISTRACTION NUMBER THREE

December 2019, Thursday morning, I'm getting ready to travel by train from London, Paddington, to Bristol, Temple Meads, for an appointment with my Australian dentist, Kain. In 2005 he helped identify the dead by their teeth after the Tsunami. I had a bad night as my psoriasis has flared up due to stress over writing this book, amongst other things. Kurt Vonnegut sucker-punched me with a quotation:

"If a person survives an ordinary span of 60 years or more there is every chance that his or her life as a shapely story has ended and all that remains to be experienced is the epilogue. Life is not over but the story is".

I can't un-know this wisdom. I will resist.

The continuing demoniacal political shenanigans have tentacled the UK and entered my dreams. A nightmare featuring a malicious senior civil servant, who drifts up like a toxic genie behind the wheel of a broad-beamed pirate ship, an unfortunate mouth that no lipstick deserves, miming the 1941 Vera Lynn hit 'White Cliffs of Dover', as the rocks come out of the mist. We've seen these people before – their bullying bluster refined through wealth and public-school entitlement should be treated with the contempt it deserves, but it isn't. I fear a subdued self-loathing populace, too cowed, too stupid, or too lazy. What will it be – could it be something else? Check out the 1950s communist witch-hunt McCarthy hearings on YouTube and watch the army lawyer, Joseph Welch, ask the bullying fraud that is Joseph McCarthy, "Have you no decency, sir, have you no decency?" Then there is that moment, that magical moment when the mist dissipates, and the spell is broken. It will happen – we just need to hold on. Hang on in there, baby...

On the outskirts of Exeter in Devon, there is a racetrack at Haldon Hill. Horatio Bottomley was an orphan brought up in Bethnal Green in the East End of London. He became a tremendous orator, a charismatic man who rose to prominence as an MP in the Liberal party during the 1900s. Bottomley was to spectacularly fall from grace through a mismanaged First World War bonds scandal. It was said he was addicted to champagne. One of his elaborate scams involved buying six racehorses, entering them in a race at Haldon Hill and telling the jockeys what order to finish in. However, the best laid plans of mice and men often go awry – a mist descended over the track and it ended in disaster. The political incompetents of now, lolloping along with no finishing line in sight, let alone an order...

Some days I'm full of confidence and others I buy into the fear. I recently watched a BBC news clip regarding the election. They were interviewing an overweight, fortyish guy in a northern food bank, asking who he would vote for. I wasn't surprised by his answer as I now feel as if I'm living in a country under occupation. People are voting against their own interests, simmering with anger that abates notionally through unnecessary purchases in huge shopping outlets and widespread littering. Ballard predicted this in *Kingdom Come*. Absolution through consumerism. It's all going on the credit cards – move it over to interest free, move it over again. Three holidays a year, Deliveroo, Amazon Prime and Netflix, a motor on lease. Vote a government in because you don't like the look of the other bloke. The northern food bank guy liked what an old Etonian had to say – an Etonian who had written disparaging articles about white working-class men – probably after mouthing disparaging remarks about black men. When I heard what he had to say I couldn't hear anything.

I feel uncertain so I post on Facebook: *Keep the faith, it's going to be just fine.* I'd wear my best clobber when I was skint sometimes. Put on a happy face like The Joker. I want to believe this.

My pal Glenn and I would sometimes phone each other up and ask, "Will it be alright?"

We'd reassure each other, "It's going to be alright". I visited the Olaf Eliasson exhibition at Tate Modern. An assertive, polite visitor assistant led us in groups of twenty through a set of white double doors into a limbo leading through to another set of double doors that opened into a corridor filled with synthetic fog lit by coloured lights.

The assistant assured us, "If you feel disorientated just look up at the ceiling, it's going to be just fine, we haven't lost anybody yet". I needed to hear that. I needed to hear a stranger tell me it's going to be alright. She also informed us the tunnel is 39 metres long, flat and straight. At that moment, I knew where I stood and I felt safe.

My dentist makes me think of Dad. I hadn't realized just how many false teeth he had – how many he was losing over the years. Within hours of his death I had cleared all his things out of the nursing home, including his pink plastic false teeth plates. Mum still had all her own teeth when she died aged 49, as sweets were rationed when she was a kid. I know the old man had lost some teeth when he was boxing but it was only a few. He'd had a gold tooth for a while. I guess I'm trying to hold on, but all the stuff that gets other people is going to get me as well. As the saying goes: *Nobody gets out of here alive.* A comforting thought when dwelling on the majority of politicians and especially their advisors.

MAMA CASS TO THE BENCH SEAT
OF A VAUXHALL CRESTA PB

"YOU SHOULDN'T BE doing that". I was in the basement of a restaurant on the harbourside in Torquay. I'm 16. I had just put my chef whites on and the woman speaking to me was a waitress nearly old enough to be my mother. I was sipping from a quarter bottle of whiskey. I didn't feel good about it and made my excuses and left. I did it again and again and again.

That particular day I had been taught by Andreas, a Greek Cypriot, to make the house speciality Boeuf a' la Greek, involving red wine and onions. I was asked by his wife Anna to deposit money at the bank – it was to support a Cypriote crisis fund, as a result of the Turkish invasion. Later I went to Jon's Boutique on the Terrace and with my wages bought a black cheesecloth shirt. I finished work, went home and wasn't able to sleep. I never knew when to call it a day as I was always frightened I was missing out on something. This will carry on right into my thirties. I probably had ADHD and as the founder of Slam poetry, the American construction worker Marc Smith, would've said, "So what!" I did read later in *The Philosophy of Andy Warhol* that 'so what' was one of Warhol's favourite stock in trade responses.

Dad had been using his left-hand drive Ford Corsair as

a minicab but got banned from driving. He was still working at the nightclub and arranged for a guy called Dai to drive on a commission basis. Dai had been in the army and was not the sharpest knife in the drawer. I met up with Dai sometime after 3:00 a.m., probably after he'd dropped Dad home, and convinced him to drive me to a local theatre where I stole a WEM amplifier. Later that morning, I sold the amplifier in Exeter. Somehow, we ended up picking up two student hitch-hikers, dropping acid with them and driving to a large shared Victorian pile in Islington. I was cool about the situation, but Dai decided to leave in order to visit a relation of his in Essex. That was the last I saw of him. It transpired weeks later that the car engine had seized up because he hadn't checked the oil. In the meantime, I had to get home to Torquay somehow. In a parallel reality I could have stayed, moved into a squat, gone to evening classes, taken a foundation course in social work, and bought a house up the road from Iain Sinclair in Hackney, or learnt a musical instrument and started a band, but I didn't. The students had given me a blanket for my journey. I got a bus to Chiswick flyover and tried to catch a ride. I decided to go to Kingston as opposed to Devon, as I had a friend, Richard LePage, who lived there. As I was standing with my thumb out, I looked down and there was a gent's watch. The pin must've come out of the strap, maybe when someone had used their arm to indicate.

I arrived in Kingston and made for the Underground as there were usually second-hand shops near stations. I sold the watch for a fiver and I noticed the *Evening Standard* news board headline: 'Mama Cass Dead'. Sherry and cigarettes would have been the order of the day then I had to set about locating Richard. How I knew his address I don't know, but eventually I found him. We went to a local primary school to meet his girlfriend, who was a teacher, and later on Richard and I went to a musical event in a fancy old house with a stained-glass front door. Apart from a piano all the instruments were handmade. Richard's instrument was a lute. It was a very civilized affair – a joint was passed around. If I were to compare this event to a band it would be the Bonzo Dog Doo-Dah Band, especially the album *Gorilla*. Richard and his girlfriend were living in one room, so I slept in a Mini outside.

The next day I hitch-hiked back down to Devon. I still had my blanket with me, and I got a lift in a Ford Capri. By late evening, I had reached Exeter and got talking to a guy with trade plates. He'd delivered a motor and was going south as well. We decided to have a kip in a car on a garage forecourt and he got us into a big Vauxhall Cresta PB with bench seats front and back. I tore the blanket in half and we took a seat each, crashing out. Back in Torquay the next day, I collected some wages owed to me and helped myself to some money from a hotel bar. I heard my dad was really worried about me, so I went down to the club where he was on the door. He was relaxed about the whole scenario and I had the impression he wasn't really bothered about the motor. His birthday was around this time and I bought him a couple of Barry White albums from the WH Smith store in Fleet Street. The shop had private booths where you could listen to records prior to purchase or just to pass the time. I bought a copy of Jethro Tull's 'Witch's Promise' from their bargain bin. I got into Pernod and *Exile on Main St.* One night, Penny, myself and another guy went nude swimming at Torre Abbey on Torquay seafront. This guy stashed his speed and lost it – he was dealing. I found it, he sorted me out, and I was up for a couple of days. Really it was a sad summer of blue Sea Dog dungarees, plimsolls and cheesecloth shirts. I was unhappy, extremely reckless, and lost.

GOING UP WEST

PORTLAND BORSTAL SHARED many of the architectural features of Dartmoor prison. I didn't experience the short, sharp shock of the detention centre. It was almost: *Go directly to jail – do not pass go*. I was 16. There were a couple of reasons for this, one being the nature of the offence, which was forging travellers' cheques. I'd go into banks with cheques usually stolen from Scandinavian students and with an English Families flight bag over my shoulder I'd ask, "You change please," and then duplicate the signature in front of the cashier. However, I came unstuck through greed. I'd acquired some £50 cheques that were stolen from, I think, a Kuwaiti. The signature would have been a bit of a challenge, but the real problem was my appearance. As much as I loved dressing up, I don't think I could've pulled off a boy Lawrence of Arabia. I made the fatal mistake of signing them and paying them into my account. During this period of recklessness, I was tearing about on a two stroke 250cc Francis Barnet, hardly Lawrence's Brough Superior. Two stroke was a mixture of oil and petrol.

There were a few other incidents: one involving assault on a taxi driver that was actually my dad's doing; and the taking and driving away of a gas board van from outside the crematorium. It was a BMC with big sliding doors. When questioned about this I said I thought the owner was dead. I was arrested and remanded in custody at Exeter. While in remand I ended up in the tractor pin workshop where Radio Two was always playing over the Tannoy. I remember an elderly actress was being interviewed and I recognized her name – one that I've now forgotten. I'd met her with Dad earlier that summer. It was a bit of a 'scouts in London visiting Buckingham Palace' moment, but I kept it to myself. There were two epileptic guys I got to know who shared a cell in the hospital wing on the ground floor. Institutions like this: built in the 1960s; locks, key chains, steel and concrete, big communal rooms, small rooms, corridors, anything off named a recess. No mystery, no character, and then no cushions or curtains, not even bath plugs. And it seemed like John Denver's 'Annie's Song' was always echoing through the landings on the Tannoy.

An escapade relating to the epileptic inmates was the main reason I was sent to Portland Borstal, as opposed to Guys Marsh, the open Borstal. They must have had something interesting about them, as I don't do boring. We would walk around the exercise yard together and casually the subject of escape had been broached – no big deal, people talked bollocks just to pass the time. I had mentioned that I had a pal who could pick me up if I got over the wall. Somehow the pair had snuck a small round-ended tractor bar out of the workshop to use as a cosh. On the appointed night, I was lying in bed fully clothed, waiting. It was probably sometime after midnight when the alarms went off and all hell broke loose, at which point I undressed and got back into bed. Early the next morning, my door was unlocked and a couple of prison officers were standing there with a long flat cardboard box containing a set of clothes. They told me to undress and put the new set of clothes on. I asked what it was about and they said it would be explained later. My new garments were grey with thick yellow stripes down the arm of the jacket and legs of the trousers.

It transpired that one of the epileptic pair faked a seizure while the other one rang the bell. A night watchman had gone into the cell but not cocked the lock – he should have shot the bolt out to prevent it from locking. One of the guys hit him and he fell back against the door and locked them all in. The whole escapade was futile, as the night watchman's key would only have opened internal doors anyway.

A senior officer explained I had been named as an attempted escapee and would be placed in isolation and two prison officers would be with me at all times. When I was taken out on exercise a book would have to be signed by the escorting officers. I was a category 'A' prisoner at 16. I denied any involvement in this escapade and never saw those guys again. When my dad and his pals visited, they thought it was a huge joke and, looking at my clothes, asked if I'd joined a band. The old man got on with the screws. They thought he was a bit of gangster through the Carlton Club association, regarding the shootings the previous December. I felt like I was playing a part in a film no one wanted to see and was stressed out at not knowing what was going to happen. The cell I was in had a raised concrete bench. In the daytime the foam mattress was taken out and at night, when I put my prison issue pyjamas on, my clothes were placed on a chair outside my cell. I remember the kindness of other lads, sneaking me tobacco and chatting through the door when they could. The day came and I was sentenced to six months to two years Borstal training.

Portland had the dubious honour during the 1960s of being the only Borstal in England where a guard and an inmate had been murdered. When I arrived at Portland there was a guy older than me (some of the inmates were upwards of twenty-one) called Richie Allen. Richie knew my dad through the nightclub in Torquay and he kept an eye on me like a big brother; but if I created problems for myself then that was my look out. Richie was adopted and his dad was a bandleader. He suggested I read T.E. Lawrence's *Seven Pillars of Wisdom,* while working in the laundry and operating an industrial press. My reading matter at this point was Sven Hassel and his tales of battles in a penal regiment on the eastern front during WWII, Dennis Wheatley's *The White Witch of the South Seas* for the sexual allure, and of course Harold Robbins for everything else. Martin from Worcester introduced me to the Sensational Alex Harvey Band and the American folk singer John Prine. The music that stands out for me after all this time is *Next* by Alex Harvey and 'Sam Stone' by Prine. Martin could be exceptionally violent but fortunately I got on well with him and we were to run a book on the Grand National using the centre-fold of runners from the *Daily Mirror.* Martin was to attack another inmate in the record room so brutally he started fitting. I was not there at the time.

One day, my dad visited me extremely drunk accompanied by his pal Colin, who wore horn-rimmed Ronnie Kray spectacles and a badly fitting single-breasted Prince of Wales checked suit. Colin, who must have been about 40, was slight of build with grey balding hair. He lived with an ear, nose and throat doctor, who was much older than him. The doctor picked up their off-licence tab on a weekly basis. I believe Colin met the doctor as a young man when he was working as a laboratory assistant in Plymouth. For a birthday present Colin had given me a book about the 1920s, with an emphasis on art deco. He also gave me some Olympia Press editions. An ex-girlfriend of mine was to take the 1920s book when she walked out years later. The doctor and Colin shared a modest terrace house separated into two living quarters. I remember a meal one evening, more of a performance really, featuring snails in garlic butter. The main course descended into alcoholic chaos, encouraged by pink gins and slurring, caustic remarks from Colin to the doctor, who was always a gentleman.

I would go to Colin's with my dad. One morning, Dad and Colin went off in the Jag and I stayed behind to sort out the doctor's breakfast of kippers. I also tied his shoelaces, as he couldn't reach. The following day the doctor was to drop dead and I was the last person to see him alive outside our circle. I'm honoured that I could perform that act of kindness for him, especially as I found a big brown bottle of opium tincture in the medicine cabinet. Routing through medicine cabinets was a productive procedure, mainly due to dieting mothers with their large bottles of Tenuate Dospan and war-damaged dads with barbiturates, such as Nembutal and Tuinal.

As the years rolled on, Colin went from bad to worse and started collecting replica guns. I met a guy in his front room selling a couple of .22 pistols from a briefcase. He wanted £180 for the pair. On a Sunday afternoon in an Ashburton tearoom, Dad and I were once offered a Spanish 12 bore – how this came about I can't remember. We had a number of tearooms we'd go to when the pubs were closed, supping spirits out of china cups with cream teas. Totnes was a favourite. Colin had a run of unsuitable lodgers, usually sourced from the bars of local boozers he frequented. He would eventually lose the house and end up as a newspaper vendor on the street, living in a caravan in the grounds of a 'Turkey and Tinsel' coaching hotel.

Even the guard told me that I could refuse my dad's drunken visit. Afterwards I don't remember any members of staff taking the piss about it, they'd seen it all before and knew the score. Dad would have brought me a drink, a sly snifter. He had damaged the car on the way up, tangling the front bumper in a fence that had to be cut off. It surprised me they made it off the causeway – a strip of road along Chesil Beach that connected Portland to Weymouth – without getting pulled by the law. The car he was driving had been won in a game of cards; it was an Austin 1100, nothing flash.

DETROIT DIESEL FLYWHEELS
AND CHERRY B ICE BUCKETS

I WAS EVENTUALLY released from Portland armed with a City and Guilds Capstan Lathe Setting and Operating certificate, a pass with distinction no less, and a train ticket marked 'change at Yeovil Junction'. A green canvas discharge bag contained my possessions: a change of clean socks, pants, and a safety shaving kit with a tube of Palmolive shaving cream. My albums were tucked under my arm and concealed in the sleeve of *Exile on Main St.* was a wrap of pharmaceutical morphine, a leaving gift from a pal. I was to find out that while I'd been away some of my friends had got into a drug called Diconal, a pink pill usually crushed and injected. These little pink pills caused absolute devastation such as abscesses and amputations due to their chemical composition. It was said they were coated in plastic. An example of the lengths a dedicated user would go to was to be found in the archive of a local Devon newspaper. In 1977, Derbyshire man John Connors was to walk into Harry Steele's chemist opposite the coach station in Torquay with an axe and request solely Diconal tablets. They engendered a passionate and dedicated following.

I'd previously been exposed to institutional living in the children's home and I actually enjoyed many elements of the

Borstal experience, especially the opportunity to make friends and gain a sense of order, as my home life had been so unpredictable. A legacy from those days is my borderline obsessive cleanliness. In the window of the office, where the guards sat doing paperwork or reading tabloids, there was a chinagraph cartoon – in the style of the cartoonist Carl Giles – of a man in a bath with flies buzzing around him and the accompanying caption, 'Grot of the week', followed by an inmate's name. Apart from my mother telling me I should, "Shake the drips off my dinkle," as the urine could stain my pants, I'd never really had any guidance about personal hygiene. In many ways, it was the establishment and girlfriends that put me right. One girlfriend, the raven-haired, Scottish Anne, who was 34 to my 18, had a habit of rigorously washing after sex – with her there was never the intimacy of basking in the glow.

In a car park prior to a job interview, a shot of amphetamine sulphate delivered through a glass and chrome syringe with a 5/8 needle provided me with a confidence beyond Devonian sensibilities, far from cream teas and farmhouse cider. Mr Parry, an ex-navy man, interviewed me for the position of a gear cutter at the engineering works located on the local industrial estate. He remarked on the Portland Training Centre accreditation on the City and Guilds certificate but gave me the job. The pay was good and the four-day week, 10-hour day, overtime Friday mornings, suited me. The factory made power take-offs, huge Detroit Diesel flywheels clamped in the jaws on a centre lathe, components engineered for the gearboxes of airport fire engines. The factory vocabulary: duckboards, coolant and swarf, micrometers and vernier gauges, the oil-stained overalls worn with steel toe-capped boots and no ear-defenders. I would soak my hands in hot water and use tweezers to remove the metal splinters from fingers and palms on bath night. Brian, the ex-merchant navy shop steward, and Ron, an old-school skilled engineer, nursed American 1940s lend-lease machines and remembered stories of Winston Churchill as a Liberal in Oldham. There was steak and kidney pie reheated for lunch; we'd sit on a wooden bench at a big table in the canteen, make tea, and read *The Mirror*. I lived on a farm in Highampton, just outside of Okehampton, with Jimmy, an old school friend whose parents owned the place but also ran a fancy goods shop in Torquay. They entrusted Jimmy with a small dairy herd.

Jimmy had a cougar tattooed on his arm and was in an on-off relationship with Penny. He'd come out with observations such as, "Weathermen should never have a surname that is the name of a county". I remember Jimmy had pestered his parents for a drum kit for his eighteenth birthday, but instead they bought him a gold half sovereign and we went out for a meal – the first time I'd eaten duck in orange sauce. We'd sometimes go drinking in spit-and-sawdust barn-sized pubs with names like the *Pretoria*. Highampton was a place where flat-capped locals, bow-legged with veins blown in turniped noses had their own cushions on worn Windsor chairs in vinegary cider houses. One particular day I was to meet Jimmy by the taxi rank near the church in Okehampton. I arrived early and bought a packet of chalk to write the name of the pub where he'd find me on the pavement in huge letters, like the time I rang a cinema in which Jimmy was watching a film and asked for an announcement to be put up on the screen asking him to phone me. I enjoyed these little antics.

Those were the days of 10cc's 'I'm not in Love', Neil Young's 'Harvest', and The Moody Blues' 'Threshold of a Dream'. During my summer factory holiday, Jimmy and I made a gentle dawn raid on a rural doctor's surgery. The metal-framed windows pinged open on a Xylonite cream-handled knife blade with a tad of screwdriver encouragement. The glass and chrome medical cabinets, their delicate slip-over latches, held prizes of ancient analgesics in ribbed blue glass bottles with rubber stoppers by Evans and Gadd of Speke, Liverpool 1934. The subtle unforgettable fragrance of alcohol wisping from potted unguents. We drove back to the farmhouse with no headlights, our cardboard box of booty in the front footwell.

Jimmy was to overdose on Pethidine. I moved to a bedsit in the town. There was a drum table in the hallway and each resident would put their rent in a separate drawer. I bought a motor from the local auction, a Princess Vanden Plas 3-Litre with a Bournemouth LJ number plate. It had some ticket and tax – not a bad runner, shiny black with a big boot, reassuringly clunking doors. The Princess was an automatic and the exhaust was blowing. When the revs kicked up and down it had an undulating drone like a WWII German bomber, but this was nothing that couldn't be put right with a baked bean tin, some exhaust bandage, and screw rings. With less than 20 miles to the gallon, I always carried some hosepipe and a can.

Eventually, I moved on from the factory and secured a job as a barman in a holiday camp on the south coast. A reduction in money and a change of view. I met a waitress there who I named 'The White Witch of the South Seas' because she was tall, thin, with long black hair, and she would do a wavy, spooky thing with her hands after a few barley wines. She was from Plymouth and liked sex in the shower. I was soon in charge of my own intimate bar located in the manor house while the rest of the camp – chalets, blue pools, and orange umbrellas – sprawled in the grounds. Pandering to a mature clientele, the camp was more of a refined experience than the usual: ABBA, mirrored flamingos, nibbles, Martini glasses, and Cherry B ice buckets; the height of sophistication with long cigarettes, sometimes the coloured Russian ones.

I became acquainted with an older couple that ran a pub in Blackheath and owned a powder-blue Ford Granada Ghia. He wore chunky rings and loud check trousers; she wore fur and white high heels. They wouldn't have been out of place at *Abigail's Party*. Late night drinking sessions and alcoholic *bon ami*. "If you are ever in London and you want a job, come and see me".

I remember the wife taking my hand and saying, "No, he means it".

An ex-policeman working as security at the camp carried out a criminal record check after one of the bar staff was rude to his daughter – a tall, horsey anorexic. While it wasn't me who had been rude, it was my past that necessitated a move and I remembered the publicans offer in London. However, I made the mistake of not phoning first. There was no job at the Sun in the Sands, Blackheath, just a couple of halves and a bit of banter. The Princess ran out of petrol a couple of miles down the road on the edge of the Heath. I slept in the motor overnight, window open a crack; waking, stiff and skint. I used the public toilets on the Heath to wash and brush up. I had a change of clothes in the green canvas Borstal discharge bag and a resolve not to return.

SHANKS PONY TO A DHSS HOSTEL
AND A PARISIAN SENTIMENT

I WAS TO walk from Blackheath Common to the West End in my brown Stead and Simpson Desert boots. The Who were playing at Charlton football ground, as most of London could hear. Later, I was to find out Penny was there. I had resigned myself that this experience was like a penitence and probably the nearest, at this point in my life, I'd ever come to letting go. I remembered the last conversation I'd had with Mum in Devon ending with, "Promise me you won't get into trouble, son". There was no way I could ask for money from either Mum or Dad, there just wasn't any.

I could hear the old man saying, "My father never gave me anything".

On my mother's side there were the relations in Battersea and my godmother lived on Lavender Sweep, Clapham Junction, around the corner from the satirical magazine *Private Eye*. I felt it would be an admission of failure if I got in touch with any of them and, of course, there would be questions. That unwritten law of keep it all in the family, don't tell anyone anything, the failing marriages, kids playing up, keep it all behind the front door.

I decided I would set out for the West End with a vague plan to get a live-in job in one of the big hotels. The act of walking is certainly top of the list when it comes to taking things for granted when you're young. Shanks's pony: the action of walking as a means of conveyance and as a necessity because you can't afford any other mode of transport. The actual mechanics of gait, the limb and body motion, and the energy cost when you've hardly got anything in your pocket: Jon Voight in the film *Midnight Cowboy* pouring sugar into Coca-Cola and eating the left-over crackers from customers plates. Necessity, energy, and motion. A car runs out of fuel, but the walking continues. In youth, so much is taken for granted: jumping off walls; diving off rocks; excessive drinking and barbiturates; smoking Sovereign and Number 10s; having casual sex with near strangers; eating Angel Delight and pub-served steak and kidney pies.

Downtown. I was, in point of fact, walking downtown. I looked at the route and I was familiar with the physical lie of the land from Blackheath into central London. Effluvia, the liquid waste and all that can be carried in it, flows down from Nobs Hill. The affluent always live on the hill. From the air quality, views, and security, there is advantage. When the wind blows, by the time the gust reaches the east the best has been had and the poor nearly always live in the east of any city. Clifton Village, Bristol, is an excellent example of this planning model. I'm going down to uptown, through New Cross, the Old Kent Road, Lambeth Road, because I want to see the Imperial War Museum and then strike out to Waterloo and over the river.

The idea of exploring locations through walking is entering the realm of fantasy, and brought to mind the Victorian adventurer Sir Richard Burton and his clandestine journey in Mecca at a time when Europeans were forbidden access on pain of death. The negotiation of place through deportment, looking the part and fitting in. I'd learnt how to carry myself on an institution landing. I knew the score. The daydreaming of the urban wanderer – daydreaming is important. I remember the actor Denholm Elliot relating this in an interview; I always believed him and never stopped daydreaming. The psychology of street choreography: the secret is not to use too many words, stay cool, and look mean, as an old pal from Stonehouse, Plymouth, once advised. Don't gawp but keep your wits about you, don't stand about with a map in your hands staring up at buildings. Remember the success of the superb Brazilian footballer Pele was partly down to his excellent peripheral vision, apparently 30% better than the average.

Waterloo, then over the bridge to the Embankment. Cardboard city. Up through the darkness that was Charing Cross. The hungry and homeless are still fed by the side of the Zimbabwean tourist office with the dusty wooden gazelles in the windows. The past started creeping back to the London days of my childhood by the time I hit Trafalgar Square. There is a black and white family photograph of my dad surrounded by pigeons, standing between my cousin and myself, holding both our hands. My cousin Lynn and I are smiling, but my dad just looks lumbered. There is a colour photo of Dad in 1978, where he's in a down-at-heel New York, Times Square. An American phone booth is behind him, and a square-faced Ford Mercury is passing on the unmaintained pot-holed road. Dad's hands are in the pockets of his overcoat and he's staring at the camera. Here, he looks comfortable, at ease with himself. I process this wide-boy illusion, but in reality, there wasn't any money – it was all props, performance, and backdrops, creating the sets that they played their parts in. Everything lurched towards the next event with nothing getting any better.

Memories as a consolation prize dragged me deeper into Soho. There was a connection between Dad and Freddie Mills, the one-time world light heavyweight champion boxer. Freddie had a nightclub on Charing Cross Road just up from Foyles bookshop. Dad had serviced Freddie's fridges in the Nite Spot and as a kid I'd met him. July 1965 he was found dead on the back seat of his Citroen DS with a sideshow rifle from Battersea funfair next to him. Soho always had a reputation mostly revolving around the sex industry and all that went with it: bent coppers, pornographers, stories in the *News of the World*, and the drug scene, especially around Piccadilly.

Michael was an Irishman and I'm not sure exactly how we met – maybe he asked for a light, maybe I asked for a light or directions. I'm not sure. The tales of Playland on Piccadilly Circus, known as the meat rack – the sexual exploitation, the tantalising Sunday red top newspaper stories creeping into the weeklies, then splashed all over them when the names and offences get big enough. Of course, no consequences for the rich and powerful, especially bent members of parliament – *plus* ça *change*. The hard-hitting Yorkshire television documentaries – like *Johnny Go Home* and *The Murder of Billy Two Tone* – told the story of the 1970s in this area graphically well. Self-appointed predatory bishops running hostels with the blessings of social services, taking up the slack government cuts couldn't handle. Nothing really changes. While I was more into a drug scene and criminality, there was a crossover with predatory sexual behaviour. I knew some girls in Torquay who used to get Randy Mandy's (Mandrax, marketed in the States as Quaaludes) from an old guy called Dirty Bertie. He'd ply them with the pills and basically take advantage and they knew this. These pills were a favourite of Bill Cosby. Another charmer like Bertie was Maurice, a crippled ex-miner. He'd employ the same ruse with the barbiturate Tuinal. There were always runaways, girls and boys, around his house. He once did time and one of the charges was for chopping up Alsatian puppies in his fireplace. He'd save his pension while inside for a big splurge on release.

It's a different light nowadays, digital LED, but then it was neon; a burning gas, splashing on a summer evening pavement, the fumes of four-star leaded petrol, mingling with the clanking diesel taxi emissions, old cooking oil, and kebabs. The scurrying gait of street people on a mission: addicts with the darting lizard tongue from stimulants – it's timeless. Mark E. Smith did it well, as did the shyster New York lawyer and mentor to ex-president Trump, Roy Cohn. The dysfunctional playing out their theatre on the streets, mostly oblivious of the conventional going about their lawful business. Michael was like a boatman steadying the bow, keeping eye contact while the waves crashed around me. People tried to hustle, hovering, "I'm a medic for the Hell's Angels,' – a bizarre phrase I've never forgotten. Busy doing nothing really, words lost in movement and then, eventually, lost in the distance – passing ships. Michael and I got talking; he was about the same height and build as me, maybe broader, with light hair, thinning on top. He wore a Harris Tweed jacket, shirt and tie, and carried a small brown suitcase. I cut to the chase: explained the motor, the looking for work, the walking into the West End. At this moment, I probably had tobacco on me and some loose change. I was stuck in London and didn't know where my next meal was coming from. Michael told me about a government DHSS hostel in Dean Street,

Soho. He said he was going to try and get a bed there that night and suggested I went along with him.

We arrived at the hostel, through the commotion, passing bars packed with punters. I had been trying not to dwell on being less than skint, nearly down and out. There was a waiting room where we sat smoking and chatting to each other. A young Scottish lad in a cheap, ill-fitting grey suit was getting a lot of attention. It turns out he was called Tommy and was the boy in the *Johnny Go Home* documentary. He'd had some casual work hanging curtains in a hotel earlier that day and was telling tales of chambermaids. There was a procedure of delousing before you got a proper shower, there might have been a television room. We did get a sandwich and a cup of tea. The sleeping arrangements were dormitories and Michael told me to put the bed legs into my shoes. In the morning, I ate the most exquisitely creamy porridge I have ever experienced and part of the deal for staying was washing some of the floors down – a duty I happily carried out.

Michael was a fount of knowledge. When he wasn't in London, he worked for the Forestry Commission or on the roads. He certainly knew how to survive in the city and this was an awful time to be Irish due to the IRA outrages that were a regular occurrence. He'd had plenty of harassment, getting stopped and searched and everything that went with it, enduring the abuse and sometimes even violence. The following day was a further education in the system. Michael explained to me that the Social Security office – where I could get money in the form of a Giro cashable government cheque – was at Scarborough Street in the East End. "Now, there could be a problem," he told me, "They will try to offer you hostel vouchers – you don't want these, or you'll be stuck here. You'll be needing to convince them you have the offer of work somewhere else like Bournemouth, and you need money for petrol".

Together we got a bus over to the East End, me carrying my little green discharge bag and Michael his brown suitcase. As we went to get off the bus, an older guy pointed at my bag and handed me a packet of 10 cigarettes saying, "I know what it's like – good luck, son". The Scarborough Street office was a performance in itself – I think it was a ticketing system and it would have been packed. I went to use the toilets where men and women were lying about all over the floors drinking booze. I was reminded of the queue and stress of pissing with my dad at a Chelsea Cup Final match in Manchester some years before. I left the Social Security office and went across the road to a block of offices to take a piss against the wall. Suddenly, I heard people banging on windows above me; I look up and realize it's a police station – the infamous one on Leaman Street. Back in the office, I was finally called and interviewed by a Polish man who took down my details.

Several hours later a list of names was read out over a Tannoy, instructing, "Come to signing box 12". I was given a Giro cheque for £15 and Michael had a result as well. We went for a couple of beers and then I headed up to Blackheath, got the can out of the boot, filled the motor, and drove back down to the south coast.

Many years later, I noticed an inscription above the door of the Shakespeare and Company Bookshop in Paris: 'Be not inhospitable to strangers lest they be angels in disguise'. I immediately thought of Michael.

DISTRACTION NUMBER FOUR

I'm on the landing getting a rain-lashing; I lock the door behind me
and head for Frying Pan Alley. It's that January winter gloom, the
cold rain, the umbrella uncertainty of will it blow inside out. The wind
whips around the 112-metre-high, 34 floor monstrosity that is the
Spitalfields Nido block, stacked with students, predominantly from
Asia and China, taking deliveries of food and drugs in their onesie
pyjamas from boys on mopeds. I walk through the lanes by way of the
Cock, the Lamb and the Crow, passing the rear of Bishopsgate police
station where the BMWs of the tactical firearms group sit waiting.
"My gang's bigger than yours".

I'm dressed in black wearing a grey woollen hat tagged with the
flag of Iceland. My soft brown Ecco boots make no sound as I walk the
elevated length of Liverpool Street station to the bus stop. I like these
boots for this particular quality, the silence. I don't wish to creep
up on anyone, it's just they offer me an illusion of youth, light on my
feet. At the terminus only a few people get on my bus. I nearly always
get my preferred seat, back left window raised platform facing the
front. Settling down, I take Orwell's 'Why I Write' out of the pocket
of my leather jacket with the enamel red star on the left-hand collar.
There was an exhibition at Tate Modern: Red Star Over Russia, in the
Blavatnik building. It was the private collection of a former Sunday

111

Times editor David King and he had generously gifted it to Tate. Soviet, Stalin era politics by way of the avant-garde; propaganda through performance and a dreadful cruelty. Pre Roy Cohn playbook, Cummings dead cat on the table.

The orangey-red roundel of Sushi Samba at Heron Tower distracts me through the condensation-feathered, rain-streaked bus window at the crossroads on Wormwood Street, Bishopsgate. It is so *Blade Runner*: the backdrop through the main drag, the channel of Bishopsgate toward Shoreditch where the 'Stage', a high-rise development incorporating the remains of Shakespeare's Curtain Theatre, offers a studio apartment on the 3rd floor for nearly 700 grand. A steel-grey sky and the vehicles beginning to morph into the shapes of 2049; they slither past their digital dashboards illuminating the black and brown tired faces of the Uber drivers. Swishing and shuddering as the motor cuts in and out, the 344 passes Threadneedle Street, then Leadenhall, down Gracechurch Street. There is an automated announcement at Fenchurch Street and then down and around the Monument. I don't like London Bridge or Borough Market, the whole area retains a darkness for me, and I don't feel comfortable there. The outrages, stabbings, and murders clag and cling to the cobbles. Both ends of the bridge have been sullied now from arse to beak. Lower Thames to Upper Thames Street tucked into the bus lane. Turning left, always left, a pathological southpaw, then over Southwark Bridge to alight near steps that take me past the demolition of the FT building.

I remember the morning after the General Election how the City workers didn't seem disappointed, they were almost jaunty in their step, while the atmosphere on my bus was heavy and people looked downtrodden. I'm sure this was not my imagination.

THE FLOWERS

RODNEY STOLE THE crochet dolly toilet roll cover from my mum's bathroom. It was a pink affair wearing a Scarlet O'Hara *Gone with the Wind* hat. The plastic doll legs went down into the roll while the dress billowed over the Andrex paper. Mum always bought Andrex as we had a golden Labrador called Cindy. All three of our dogs over the years were called Cindy. Rodney Bendix was the dolly thief, a drinking crony of my dad. He ran a prepared vegetable business supplying restaurants, local schools, and hospitals. The sort of people Dad brought home were predominately misfits, at best unconventional businessmen, full of pub crawl laughter and one-liners but they were characters. They all had stories. I suspect Rodney was roped in purely for his financial contribution towards the booze, or petrol for my dad's Jag. I could tell he wasn't hardcore, more of a blow-in. His business and marriage were crashing and the dramatic backdrop of association with my dad and his pals somehow filled a vacuum. Rodney could get over-familiar in his cups, a little too much hands on – not knowing if he was fish or fowl. He possessed a really unattractive loping gait, as if he'd never quite got used to walking upright.

The roll call of the front room drinkers was never ordinary. Tug Wilson, a second engineer – small and wiry, bearded, originally from Newcastle – was always sailing under a Panamanian flag.

He was a self-exiled shipboard saver, blowing everything on shore leave way before Tom Waits ever sang about it. There was some sort of arrangement, to Tugs advantage, between my dad and Gladys, the bouffant, black-winged glasses-wearing taxi controller, involving sexual favours. Tug died, apparently drunkenly crushed between his ship and the dockside, still owing my dad money. Then there was Dougie Kip, who had once competed in a 1960s 24-hour Le Mans and a number of other racing competitions. He was quietly amusing and somewhat sly, as if he was always checking in the rear-view mirror. Dougie had a business importing fancy goods specifically from the Philippines and was married to a successful hairdresser. The showman Tony Pelmet could light up the room and had a catchphrase: "*It's nice to be nice*". He had a fabulously detailed tattoo of a fox disappearing up his arse and could play piano, tell jokes, and was proud of his traveller heritage. His wife would leave him because of his violent temper. Tony was muscled, bunchy, and nimble; he'd run a couple of pubs for the Greek Cypriot owner of the Carlton Club, who my dad had once worked for arranging door security. Tony was somehow holding on. Ronnie Flexor, the one-time tennis pro and trainer to the Las Vegas bodyguards of reclusive Howard Hughes, had bloodshot eyes and tiny burst capillaries spidering his nose, spreading onto his cheeks like a Venetian mask. Occasionally he could be seen giving a few lessons at the corporation-run tennis courts near the park. Most of Ronnie's income now came from the rents of a house he had converted into bedsits. There was a distant, sad divorce and disputed family money, but these never got in the way of a good afternoon drinking session. It wasn't just the drink that united these misfits; what they all had in common was they were either leaving or had been left by their partners, lovers, and wives.

While this drinking camaraderie was very entertaining for Dad and his cronies, it must have been really tedious for my mum. I don't think she had the energy to resist. The monotony of hearing Burt Bacharach's soundtrack from *Butch Cassidy and the Sundance Kid,* Johnny Cash's *Live in San Quentin* or Sinatra's double album *Portrait of a Man* must have been exhausting, along with Dad getting out his scrap book and reliving highlights from his boxing days in the 1950s – the 'could-have-been's – and the drunken phone calls to old pals in The Smoke, like Terry Downes, the one time world middleweight champion with the fabulous sobriquet of 'Tearaway Terry, the Paddington Express'.

Nothing was conventional, everything revolved around pub and club hours, the who, what's and when's, and the means to be continually drinking. Mum was really quite ordinary and just trying to get through this madness with her Mills and Boon books, Amitriptyline and red Embassy cigarettes. I was aware of that and ashamed of my part in this drunken parade. In the last pub my dad had run, a decade previously, he used to cavort about with his pals while Mum did all the work. She took pills because of an earlier cerebral haemorrhage, possibly brought on by stress and hard work. What had been the purpose of them leaving London for a better life in Devon? It struck me that Dad had managed to isolate Mum from her family so he could continue partying on his terms. There was a little more to it and Dad had always insisted that Mum had been exploited by her family. Being the eldest daughter, her father Harold expected too much of her, especially after Nanny Lillian had died. While there might have been some truth to this, it was almost as if he was taking over Harold's role and instead of looking after Mum and providing safe sanctuary, it was constant drama and an open house. I can still catch myself saying, "Poor old mum," as I make pilchards on toast.

Ruby Murray, the 1950s Irish chanteuse, came around to our house one night for a meal with her husband Ray Lamar. Ruby lent me a book about Edith Piaf, the Sparrow of Paris. Her story appealed to my melancholic, alcohol-drenched mindset. Piaf's great love was a professional boxer called Marcel Cerdan, a French Pied Noir, born in Algeria during French occupation. I tried to romanticize what was clearly a dysfunctional relationship between my parents. The illness Mum had endured over the years had left her almost too delicate to significantly hug. There had been times when everything seemed terrific, like dancing with her to Mud's 'Tiger Feet' in The Union, a local pub, and once in the front room she'd tried to teach me to waltz. Dancing had been a brief manifestation of celebration between us – trying to tell each other something. I knew that we both wanted a different life. But the truth is I didn't know her that well.

Mum's front room had a three-piece white leatherette sofa with orange cushions. A cocktail cabinet matched the table and four chairs, bought when she was married in Battersea circa 1955. There was a 1970s swirling carpet, with a white sheepskin rug in front of the wall-mounted gas fire. In the display section of the cocktail cabinet was a tea set I'd bought for her from Lawleys in Fleet Street, Torquay, in 1973. Uncle George, who was torpedoed twice during the Second World War, married to Auntie Beat, and rode a 650 BSA with a bullet sidecar, had given Mum a stainless teapot and coffee jug with sugar and milk accessories on a matching tray. There were also a few crystal glass pieces from Scandinavian

EF students who had experienced the lunacy that passed as our home. I was particularly fond of a brown-bodied Rynbende fawn ornament from one of Dad's pubs, the rotten little cork in its neck still smelling of cherry brandy. There was a sweet indefinable smell to the cabinet. The cocktail section came down on stuttering metal arms and a white-braided thin wire connected to a small strip light that didn't work anymore. A brass sunburst electric clock shared the wall with a praying hands reproduction sketch and two miniature white busts of Wellington and Napoleon. I took notice of the little things Mum liked and collected – her small comforts. The wicker shopping bag with the centred flowers on each panel and the lemon sweets, leaching their sherbet, stuck to the plastic lining. The scrunched, lace-edged hankies with embroidered roses, that she used to lickety spit and wipe chocolate from my little boy chops. These were her small tokens of self-reward, because Dad certainly never bought any little surprises home, or at least nothing she welcomed. This is why I recognised Mum's crochet dolly in Rodney's bathroom. I could imagine Rodney giving the toilet roll holder to his wife in a pathetic drunken grand gesture. It was his limit.

I was to work for Rodney, an arrangement that suited my dad (at my expense) very well. His premises were located amongst a hotchpotch of buildings housing a vending machine supplier, ice cream van storage, and a small electrical repair business run by a Polish ex-RAF radio operator. These were stables and farm buildings that had been converted and, in the case of Rodney's unit, badly. The farm had long gone, gobbled up with post-war social housing. An old inn displaying horse brasses and copper bedpans with a low-beamed bar had survived and was still servicing the area. Across the road from the unit was a cluster of small cob cottages with thatched roofs. I could imagine cream teas and roses round the door. A John Hinde colour-saturated postcard moment.

It was an old building and the constant cold made me angry, compounding the grim realization that this is what happens when you don't do well at school – no laughing at the back of the class now – just hammering home the self-doubt and self-loathing. Not much encouragement was needed for another serious glug of spirits in this near-derelict factory stinking of fermenting vegetables and stale tobacco. The once white walls were speckled with damp and the strip lights would regularly flicker before the electrics tripped out. It had a tin roof and mostly bare concrete floor, apart from duckboards around the large plastic sinks that were like half-barrels on their sides. There was a tall Dickensian desk and lectern with a sloping top just inside the front door. I'd found a framed sepia photograph of a Victorian dignitary amongst a box of tat, his hands holding the lapels of a morning coat. I put it up on the wall by the desk and chinagraphed across it: 'Our Founder'.

The potatoes and carrots, sometimes turnips or parsnips, were emptied into the industrial peeling machines. The potatoes came in brown heavy-duty paper 56 pound bags, half a hundredweight. They were usually tied at the top with twisted wire, which had to be wiggled up and down and around until it snapped. Swinging the bag up onto my shoulder and removing a rubber lid about the size of a seven-inch single, I'd tip the potatoes into the revolving drum which was coated in an abrasive material that removed the skin from the vegetables. Sometimes there would be stones and I'd have to stop the machine and remove them as they could get wedged in the undulating spinning plate at the bottom. Once peeled, I'd open a lipped gate and the potatoes would tumble out into a plastic dustbin. They'd then be transferred to the plastic troughs to remove eyes and blemishes before cutting to shape. Prior to bagging up for delivery they would be soaked in Drywite, a chemical that kept them looking white in the plastic bags.

It was necessary to work nights in order to have the vegetables prepared and ready for the following morning when Bob and his pal Eric would turn up in their blue Triumph 2000 for the deliveries. Bob and Eric were a visually striking pair. Bob was short, broad, and wore a pork pie hat, whereas Eric was about six foot four and eighteen stone. He always did the top button of his shirt up – in the mid-seventies I don't think we were as casual. I recall standing on the corner outside The Union pub one night waiting for them to give me a lift to the factory. I'd see them coming towards me, their heads backlit by the streetlights. Bob's head would be just above the steering wheel and Eric's wedged up against the roof lining. I'd get in the back and create a gentle gradation with my own head between the seats chatting to them.

Some nights I'd as good as demolish a 40 oz bottle of vodka. I had a deal with a barman of a local Conservative club. I'd met him the previous year working at the same holiday camp where Ruby was appearing; he'd steal the booze and I'd buy it from him. I would use anything really as long as it was furiously mood altering, I could still function, and it didn't involve hallucinations.

Bob the driver hadn't been paid and there was the continuing delicate situation of my dad drinking with the main culprit. There was a visit from Environmental Health and then the changing of vegetable suppliers with various people, in particular the landlord, turning up asking for Rodney. Everything revolved around money.

I did manage to get some money from him one night in The Fortune of War, but in the hustle of palmed notes and drunken bonhomie he short-changed me a fiver. I could tell Dad was getting bored with him and his incessant mithering about his low-cal domestic situation. Criminality was always more appealing to the old man's crew; it was either not guilty or doing time, rarely anything in-between. And whatever the outcome, there was always an excuse to drink, bringing on tearful macho sentimentality from men who couldn't provide for their own. I suspect Rodney thought association with my dad offered him some protection from creditors, particularly if he was getting the drinks in. There was a confrontation one night at The Queens Hotel on the Strand in Torquay. Bob drove me over there and went into the bar and kicked off at Rodney – as expected the old man took Rodney's side. I can't recall exactly what I said but Dad chased me out. I rapidly jumped in the motor, Bob floored it, and we barely missed running him over.

I was determined not to let Rodney off the fiver. I had a friend whose parents ran a hotel on Babbacombe Downs opposite the theatre. I'd worked there during school holidays years before. I knew my friend was now managing the hotel, so I gave him a bell, asking if he was interested in buying a hundredweight of potatoes – there had been a serious drought the year before and potato prices were still high. I fetched two bags from the unit and carried them in relay to a bus stop, probably a quarter of a mile away. I had to change buses on the Strand; I seem to remember someone helping me from one bus to the other. The final bus took me to Babbacombe, and I relayed the bags to the hotel, which was situated about 200 yards from the bus stop.

At one point on this escapade I recall experiencing the 'Trevor taste' – it usually manifested itself under stress and must have been brought on by my exertion. The Trevor taste also happened at a garage in Lisburne Square that Ronnie Flexor's family had once owned when it was a British Leyland dealership. When I was about 11 years old and my mum had been in Freedom Fields Hospital in Plymouth recovering from a haemorrhage, I'd stayed with an elderly couple that had a café at Lisburne Square. I would go over to the garage and the forecourt attendant would sometimes let me work the pumps.

Needless to say, myself, Bob, and Eric were never short of prepared vegetables, but it was hard cash we needed, Bob for household expenses and me probably to waste on drink and drugs. We all knew this wasn't going to end with a gold watch or even a half-civilized night out with the boss. Looking back, this situation was preparation for how everything turned out over the next twenty years. It was extreme, no half measures – straight from the bottle. Between us we hatched a plan that involved pre-empting when Rodney would normally collect the dues from the restaurants (there was no billing, just cash in hand). I then went in with the deliveries and asked for cash on the spot. I've always been very plausible so most of them paid up and we carried on until we reached the amount that Rodney owed us. I don't think we took a liberty. We all had a laugh about it, but I was the one with wet feet in a freezing factory glugging out of a bottle at four o'clock in the morning, knowing this was fucked up.

I walked to the local Co-op with my dues and bought a bunch of flowers and a box of Milk Tray chocolates for my mum together with a quarter bottle and some cigarettes for myself. There is a scene in the film *One Flew over the Cuckoo's Nest* where Chief Bromden, the Native American Indian, relates to Randle, the character played by Jack Nicholson, about how his father had been an alcoholic and he 'watched the bottle suck the life out of him'. At this point in my life, I felt that swig was fuelling me and getting me through. "I'll sort it out – pull myself together, plenty of time…" Burying it deeper, drinking and using more, the behaviour more extreme and the consequences, yes, the consequences…

DISTRACTION NUMBER FIVE

On Mondays, I attend a reading group at Second Home just off Brick Lane. It's one of those uber-trendy start-up gaffs: hot-desking shared spaces, entrepreneurs, and the like. A fair percentage of the guys are bearded, wear shoes with pop socks, and sport tortoise-shell spectacles like those of Harvard academics. Always spectacles, never glasses. The partition walls are Perspex, the chairs are mix and match shabby functional, and the bases of the tables are fashioned from industrial concrete- reinforcing steel. There is free tea but, compared to Nude, substandard coffee, and a selection of milks, mindful of the lactose-intolerant. All this is dispensed from kidney-shaped beverage islands fitted with instant boiling water taps. Second Home also runs a bookshop across the road. I tried to get my book *Smoke and Other Tales* in there but they wouldn't have it – they were more interested in getting Will Self, who wrote the foreword. Times like that, I felt like an old-fashioned boy – an out of date boy. The guy I spoke to wore high-end spectacles.

Our group takes turns in reading and discussing short stories and poems, our entrance fee paid for by the Royal Literary Fund. A prize-winning female novelist of mostly historical romantic fiction runs the group. She reminds me of a Joanna Hogg character, and I take cues from the films *Archipelago* and *Souvenir* on how to respond.

I revert to a type of Peter Sellers character, specifically Chance the gardener in the movie *Being There*. I imitate a behaviour that I think is required and my reference is usually from a film. I find myself witness to quiet considerations before she asks someone's opinion on, say, a brutal Betjeman war poem.

All the time there is an oscillating hum of activity around the borders of our see-through room; people talking into black spidery conference call devices that squat on the tables like little spaceships. The constant chatter... I'd listen for clues regarding political affiliations in what was for me a passionate and sensitive time. I heard references with more than a little affection to 'Boris', by women of a certain age. I realized I'd have to change my tone.

I did read one of the prize-winning novelists' books set in the art world of 1990s London. I ordered it through Abe books, and had it sent to the Welsh address. I noticed there was a great deal of fucking by numbers in this particular book and interestingly no oral sex. I did mean to ask her why this was the case. I had read somewhere – I think it was Charles Bukowski – who said he considered oral sex to be cheating, but not in a Bill Clinton get-out clause sort of way. I think he was alluding to the friction of penetration, that self-control, working at the edging. As an aside, Jonathon Meades said he always thought of Princess Anne when he wanted to delay orgasm.

When I called into Nude coffee in Hanbury Street for my double macchiato on my way to the group, I'd often see Damian Lewis sitting at a window seat with a woman. He always looked slightly quizzical, as if he was about to say something. I think perhaps it was to do with his overbite. I'd seen him around Spitalfields a few times. I found him extremely convincing in *Homeland* and particularly good in the spy film *Our Kind of Traitor*. He is a man naturally suited to spectacles.

Over the years, he has grown on me and I'm tempted to give him a copy of my book *Lubin Tales*, stressing he'd have to pay for *Smoke and Other Tales* though.

Louise and I stayed in a Hussmann-designed apartment near St Denis, Paris, some years back. It belonged to a friend of mine who worked in the City of London. Chris and his wife plus two daughters holidayed at my apartment in London, while we stayed in their magnificent Parisian pad with parquet floors and full-length windows opening out onto the boulevard. He had thoughtfully left a bottle of champagne in the fridge with various cheeses. His wife was the manager of a beauty spa whose clients included the late Olivia De Havilland. During our stay, we noticed an unusually large number of different styles of spectacles scattered throughout the apartment. We photographed these in situ and presented Chris with a small booklet of our ocular documentation.

I never did change my tone to accommodate the Johnson groupies and as a New Year resolution I stopped attending the class. I did miss seeing Damian Lewis in Nude, but that was all really.

THE TATTOOIST'S SMACKED WHITE JAG

THE QUEEN OF the English Riviera, one sleepy summer Sunday afternoon all sun and seagull feedback, I get a call from Roger, "All right, how's it going? Gerry, can you sort out some Billy for the Major and I'll sort you some of the other at mine?" The 'other' I knew would be gear, smack, or morphine and probably pharmaceutical. This is Devon 1980 and it's easier to turn a chemist over than score opiates. The Billy was a reference to Billy Whizz – speed. My pal Regan is with me; he is partial to a drink, frequently, and wouldn't say no to some speed. The pubs close at 2pm Sunday and reopen at 7pm; left between the devil and the deep blue sea for those of us who never know when to stop. Lunchtime darts, roast potatoes, cheese and pineapple on the bar...

There are a few off-licences that will sell alcohol out of hours and I'd found one in a row of terraces, run by South Koreans. One afternoon, in the offy, I happened to notice the edge of a piano poking out of the stockroom door. It turned out the previous owners had left it. Running my fingers along the keys, I checked they all worked, taking the panel off above the pedals. It was a steel-frame overstrung – the longer the strings, the better the sound and good resale value. I asked them if they wanted to sell it. I rang Paul F. who had worked with my dad in a casino in Torquay. Paul F. was a very lucky man. He'd had a loaded gun pointed at him in the

1973 incident; the gunman had already shot a policeman before he arrived at the casino. Paul had somehow managed to swerve this. He was married to a woman twenty years younger than him and was now driving a taxi with a side line in buying and selling. It was always easy to get in touch with pals who drove taxis because they had radios. He came to the offy, paid them, and I got a finder's fee. But that was another Sunday, not the tattooists smacked white Jag Sunday.

Roger was quite a formidable guy. He usually wore a double-breasted pinstripe suit, occasionally with a pork pie hat. He had a Popeye Doyle/Gene Hackman mien, fast glance agility with a Devonian accent. Roger could talk a hungry cat off the back of a fish truck. The Major was a different ball game: short, squat, and balding, with a touch of Dickie Attenborough. He was one of the Brighton Boys, an old friend of my dad from the club days. An antique dealer in the sense he sold antiques, but how he acquired them was something else. The devious tactics to get through the front door, from glossy leaflets offering appraisals by companies with stately sounding names like Grosvenor or Balmoral, alluding to a royalist respectability that appealed to the older clientele, who possessed tea trays and biscuit barrels with Her Majesty's image on. Then there were the variations on the 'Swedish beetle', creating holes in furniture and skirting boards with a dart, or spraying with water to give the impression of dampness. This fictitious domestic invasion, when creatively explained to the elderly homeowner, would generally have the desired effect of justifying the removal of the affected object in order to implement a procedure that would eliminate the beetle. This would also involve a mixture of convincingly smelling chemicals sprayed at random locations with great ceremony inside the property. I always suspected there was some element of Stockholm syndrome partnering these dealings. Relationships based on loneliness, one-sided financial reward, and throw in a touch of the craic. Individuals like the Major in their blazers, the wire crest faded and tarnished, were very plausible. They knew how to read people. There were occasionally return visits and items put on the 'mace' meaning they were talked out the door, put through auction, and paid for later out of the sale. Usually, it was only after a rapacious relation noticed an item of furniture was missing that the police would get involved. It is generally accepted that most antiques have been stolen at least once in their lives.

Memory is a strange thing. There are weeks, months, huge parts of years where I don't remember much, the sort of years where a David Bowie album slipped by unnoticed, or a series of space-themed films were released. This is not because I was in a black out or it was so traumatic – I just couldn't be bothered. Content to just sleepwalk through a beige existence of apathy, with my black Samsonite bag filled with works, wine, and a rarely entered notebook over my shoulder. This particular Sunday however lodged in my memory, probably because some of these individuals accompanied me through significant and dark days over the years. 13 years later one of these characters was to be instrumental in me sorting myself out. In a narrow alley, under a concrete streetlight with a bare bulb and a round chrome reflector, similar to the one in Picasso's *Guernica*, Denis was there at the right time, with the right words.

Regan and I were out in the garden reading the papers and enjoying the sunshine when Roger phoned; my girlfriend would have been at her mothers. My landlord Albert took the call on the payphone in his hallway. We had a really cool flat in a smart area – the bedroom windows overlooked Cockington Meadows. It was near the seafront but just far enough away from town to deter people from popping in unannounced. I remember when we went around to view the place Albert had pointed at a stack of letters on his sideboard that were responses to the advert. I discovered later that the neighbours were for the most part insufferable snobs. One morning, I found a handwritten note under my windscreen wiper requesting I didn't park my Transit outside as it lowered the tone of the neighbourhood. Or words to that effect.

Regan and I got in the motor, picked some booze up from the Koreans, scored some speed, then drove over to Roger's. A white 1973 XJ Jaguar on an N-plate was parked outside. The car had been pranged on the driver's side front wing, affecting the tracking. If you took your hands off the wheel the car would pull to the left. Roger's house was on a neat but narrow tree-lined road of mixed council and private housing. A school friend of mine had lived next door to Roger before he went off to join the army. His sister had written sick notes for me to enable my truancy years:

Dear Miss Davie,
Gerry has been off school this past week due to scarlet fever…
Yours sincerely, Mrs King.

Paul C. had bought the Jaguar from Vincent Shed, a tattooist whose parlour was on a steep hill located near Warren Road – an address referred to as 'Heroin Heights' by local taxi drivers. The legendary South West tattooists Les Skuse from Bristol and Doc

Price, Plymouth, were his artistic contemporaries: skin brightly inked with Japanese gardens and Vargas-inspired women adorning the nose cones of fighter-bombers. At one time, the majority of guys getting inked were servicemen or criminals, there really wasn't much in between. I think heavy metal might have brought in new punters. Tattooing never appealed to me, I reckoned fingerprints were enough.

Regan and I go into Roger's and Regan starts chatting with Roger's missus Chippie, who likes a drink. Chippie always reminded me of a Devonian version of Cilla Black. I'm introduced to the Major and give him the speed. He chops it out on an LP cover of the *Massed Pipes and Drums of the Scottish Highlands* while his pal Dean, average height, slight, a bit of the Gary Numan about him, is rolling a note into a tube in anticipation. The Major looks up at me as he passes the speed to Dean and says, "Give my regards to your father".

Roger motions me into the kitchen, "Now – Denis is coming around and he's not to know anything about this – especially this," pointing at Paul C., who is cooking up gear in a spoon over the stove. "For fuck's sake, don't mention the speed either". Paul is a little over six-foot; Daniel Craig would be a good comparison. He has a weird sort of reverse laugh, like he's breathing it back in. Not that we're laughing now, nobody wants to spill anything. This is serious business.

At this point, the front room is a booze and speed zone, but no one is to know we are doing morphine in the kitchen. For Denis' benefit, there were no drugs involved at all. The thing is with the booze, get enough of it down and nobody picks up on what is going on in any case. The morphine is pharmaceutical and strong like hobnail boots tramping all over you, as opposed to the slippers of smack. We are sweating – shirts off, bent double – until it levels out. Then back into the front room – by now the personalities are coming out. Roger is up on a charge relating to beating a nightclub doorman with a chair leg. He starts to discuss the finer points of this incident while the Major nods intently, doing the Mark E. Smith speed-tongue thing. Dean is in the kitchen and finds a tea towel that he puts over his head like a judge's wig. He points to Roger, who is perched on the edge of the settee, facing the Major, saying in his posh boy voice, "I can see no alternative other than a custodial sentence – you will go to prison for two years – take him down".

Roger responds, not missing a beat, but with slightly nodding eyes and a sly nose rub, "You don't know what the fuck you're on about – if you look at the witness statement…" We're all saved by the bell as Denis is now at the door, slicked-back black hair, tattooed knuckles, and wearing his favourite brown leather jacket with a black shirt and white tie, even though it's summer. He pecks Chippie on the cheek. He's having a Bacardi with coke. Regan and Chippie top up and, to be polite, mine is a couple of fingers with a splash.

Roger has very blue eyes with tiny pinned pupils. In the film *The Man with the Golden Arm*, there is a scene where a guy asks the main character Frankie Machine, played by Frank Sinatra, for a light. Sinatra sparks his Zippo and the guy uses the flame to illuminate Sinatra's heroin pinned pupils, proving the point he was using again. Roger didn't want Denis to get too close so with gesturing introductions and a smile, he says to me, "Gerry, come and get those curtains out the van". I follow him outside to his

Transit and in the back are some heavy gold velvet curtains I'd lent him to wrap some furniture in. We take them out of his van and throw them in the back of mine. "You got anything in the auction, Ger?" The auction Roger is referring to is based in Exeter – I'd mentioned his name and been welcomed into the fold of cash up-front payments on the reserve price of the goods coming out the back of the van. The brown-coated porters carried the gear into the auction rooms and the auctioneer wrote up the list.

"Yep, Thursday – mahogany drop-leaf table, it's down as George III – it's in the antique sale, should make a few quid". The antique sale as opposed to the general furnishing was always where I wanted to be.

"Is it from the clearance up Wellswood?" I answer yes. Palming me a wrap of morphine, he says, "Here's a little something for later, Ger".

"Ah, just what the doctor ordered!" I reply, slipping it into the watch pocket of my Levi's.

"Wasn't it a doctor's gaff, the clearance?" I nod in agreement. Roger laughs, "That Dean can be a twat – you've got to watch him. You know he got Bruce Woolley nicked". This had happened in a hotel restaurant that was well known for serving alcohol after hours to people who weren't guests. The police had raided the place and Dean had thrown a lump of hash under the table, but it landed right under Woolley's chair. Bruce Woolley had a hit in 1979 with 'Video Killed the Radio Star' and this bust was to make his life difficult when applying for a visa to tour the States.

Obliquely, the clearance in Wellswood at 'Westwick' was a stroke of luck. Regan had lived there as a lodger. Returning home one evening from his work as a furniture salesman at Williams &

Cox, a bespoke family store, he found his landlord Doctor White dead. Regan moved out some time after that and went to live with his stepmother. Quite a number of his possessions were still in the apartment and he'd arranged for the doctor's solicitor to take him in there and collect them. I went along with Regan, suggesting it must be heart-breaking to leave so many items that held fond memories and offered to buy the entire contents. The solicitor asked if I would like to name a sum – we'd already had a good look around. An appointment was made at his office, we agreed on a slightly higher figure, signed the paperwork, and bought the contents. Cash, of course.

The entrance to Westwick was through a heavy glass-topped front door. The rooms leading off to the left were windowless, while on the right French windows looked out onto a shrubbery and a lawn. The treatment room at the end of the hallway was well lit and bright. Doctor White was an osteopath. Regan had a great deal of respect for him and was genuinely saddened by his death. His apartment had been left to a relation living in Paris who couldn't be bothered to come and sort his personal possessions out. It wasn't an age or infirmity issue, it was just apathy.

I'd be a liar to say the sale was just business. I had a genuine interest in many of the artefacts: clues to a life in the knick-knacks, photographs, and correspondence – small details connecting to bigger stories. A few items of furniture more than paid for the clearance. There was also a low-mileage Japanese car in the garage, a Mazda with a rotary Wankel engine. There were two daggers hanging in the hallway, one was a WWII German navy Kriegsmarine and the other Luftwaffe, German air force. These we advertised through the personals in the *Daily Telegraph*. The history of 'Westwick' revealed itself as we were clearing it. Doctor Bill White had known Stephen Ward of the Profumo scandal, possibly because Ward's father was the vicar of St Matthias church on nearby Babbacombe Road, but more likely through his professional capacity as an osteopath. Ward had practised for a while in Torquay.

The days of cheques and paying extra for express clearance... A mahogany George III drop-leaf table had been concealed under an inlaid octagonal Victorian table-top covered with a drape. Looking like instruments of torture, the doctor's extremely heavy, beige-toned, metal osteopathic treatment apparatus had to be taken to the tip. We'd put word around but there were no takers. Nikki, an eccentric Russian ex-ballet dancer, called in to enquire about the piano. Nikki lived in a mews flat in Wellswood village with a steep narrow staircase leading to small servant quarters above a garage. There was no way the piano would fit in his gaff. I had been introduced to Nikki by a friend who had bought a Tuxedo from him and played bass guitar for the support band of many of the stars performing at the summer theatres in Torquay. Nikki wore a hearing aid and was thickset with a fine head of bouffant hair. He was often loud and excitable, causing his ear snail to squawk.

Another unconventional individual was 'Mad Madge', who we came across while carrying out house clearances. She was a magistrate who ran an antique shop. The first time she did business with us she had to be assured that we were *bona fide* by the solicitor we'd obtained the house clearance through. Madge was tall, thin, and wore big floppy hats and floaty dresses, a Joanna Lumley without the skin tone. Regan would often sweat profusely and she'd think it was because he'd carried a tea chest full of bric-a-brac into the shop. The usual reason was that he'd had a skinful the night before and was probably speeding. Madge would then fix him Lemon Barley water and insist he sat down. She did get some decent stuff from us though: Hitler Youth annuals and a number of photograph albums – a world tour during the 1930s with pyramids, desert scenes, North Africa, and nubile tribesmen. There were also some watercolours of Menton in the south of France.

OPIUM, P4 ROVERS, ANNE SUMMERS
AND THE NORTH CIRCULAR

OUR SOUNDTRACKS OF that summer were The Rolling Stones' *Emotional Rescue* and Bob Seger and the Silver Bullet Band's *Stranger in Town*. Summers that went on and on, jumping in hotel pools fully clothed, cars that started first time, and always money for meals out. I'd discovered opium through a pal from Manchester, who I first met when he was a glass collector in the Yacht pub on the seafront. He was murdered back in Manchester in the early 1990s. I went through a phase of popping a generous plug in the French tradition; shades of *The Quiet American*. Leisurely evenings spent walking from hotel bar to hotel bar – some had piano players in the lounge with names like Spike. Drinking chilled orange juice in tall glasses placed on puffy, embossed paper doilies.

There would be interludes of reasonable ordinariness when we'd go out into the countryside and visit a friend of mine, a solicitor's son, who lived in a Tudor manor house complete with banqueting hall. It was the first time I'd seen a vitrine outside of a museum. His grandmother would sit outside his younger sister's room on a nursing chair reading bedtime stories and there were darts in the body of a painted face grandfather clock. His summer job was working at a film processing lab and he had a collection of confiscated smut. Looking through this carpet-concealed grubby collection, I recognized a smiling ex-Carlton Club waitress resplendent with an intimately placed Babycham bottle.

One night I took some photographs with a co-worker when I worked nightshift years later in Oxford. Small forklift trucks badged 'Climax' scooted around the factory transporting motor parts. There were signs on the walls warning: 'Beware of Climax'. My colleague snapped me pointing to one of these signs with my hand on my crotch. When the images came back from the processors the word 'Climax' had been scratched out on the negative. I would wager whoever was responsible for that never had a grandmother reading them bedtime stories.

It's August bank holiday, Anderton and Rowland fairground is on Torre Abbey meadows, and John is out of Physeptone amps. "Let's go up to London and score – go and see Jay, you up for it?" he asks. Yeah, what the fuck. The three of us pile into the Transit and Regan takes a turn driving. Chris Petit's *Radio On* is a stand-alone example of a British road movie. American road movies can simply play a soundtrack and pan vistas of New York City from a helicopter, downtown Vegas, or the Hollywood Hills. All the good stuff in the UK is dreamt up in the suburbs like the world of J.G. Ballard between his school runs or Keith Richards immortalising his West Sussex gardener in the ultimate driving track 'Jumping Jack Flash'. We just don't have the scale and distance. Slow motors: sedate on A roads, struggle on motorways. The Jag in *Withnail and I* slouches out of the city with McGann piloting and Richard E. Grant hurling abuse from the wound-down window. A 1967 V4 Transit is probably on performance par with Petit's late 1950s P4 Rover struggling from Bristol to London. There was nothing smooth about driving a P4 Rover, no power-assisted steering, the regal gear changes. In 1973, the house master from Fullaford drove me to the dentist in his Rover. The car was old then and the conversation stilted.

Gas up, packets of cigarettes, cider, wine – there would've been rough packing blankets and curtains for wrapping furniture in the back of the van. A woman I knew had given me some Filon and Mandrax, part of a trade-in on some furniture from the Westwick clearance. The suppressor wasn't working on the radio and the buzz took the boredom out of the journey. London, over the Westway and into the West End. Parking the van up around Dean Street, we leave the bonnet open for the benefit of traffic wardens. Jay works in an Anne Summers shop near Raymond's Revue Bar in Berwick Street. Jay hasn't got any gear; John sells him some gold jewellery. We walk off to Piccadilly, giving a quid to some guy who tells us who's holding. Three nectarines for a pound on the Dilly, kebabs and souvenirs. Eros watches over black cabs, Red Routemaster buses, and assignations. *If you stay on Piccadilly long enough, you'll meet everyone you ever knew.* We score Diconal, Ritalin and Diamorphine dry amps. I had a concern with London tap water, so I bought bottled – it turned out to be fizzy, of course; I didn't use it. We shoot up in the van in Hyde Park. It's a series of fast edits on a hot day – the day is empty but for the rushes and every cigarette. We crash out in the van; I wake up early and drive over to Smithfield meat market. The pubs are open from about 6 a.m. for the porters and you can tell the Old Bill by their shoes. I sneak into a nearby hotel and get a shower.

Later, driving out on the North Circular somewhere along the A406 we hit a traffic jam and we're elevated looking down into the cars either side. John tells me to put my arm back over the seat and he shoots me up with a cocktail of Diconal and Ritalin. It feels like my head is going through the roof. Later, as we motor down to Devon, I start hallucinating – a side effect of the active ingredient Cyclizine in the Diconal. It's going to be variations on a theme for a decade or so.

DOLL WITHIN A DOLL

ONE NIGHT, I went with some pals to The Casino, a huge seafront pub, in Paignton. I entered a yard of ale competition in a Courage beer promotion night and won. I was presented with a tankard and prize beer vouchers by the England 1966 World Cup winning football captain Bobby Moore. I read years later he was doing this work because he needed the money. He came across as a really decent man and it must have been demeaning for him having to put up with drunken fools' night after night. I did it for the free beer and felt stupid with my picture on the front page of a local newspaper the next week. I had the tankard engraved with the names of the pals I was with that night and left it in a laundrette I'd sheltered in, drinking. 'What Do You Want From Life?' – that party favourite from those American funsters The Tubes, hot outta San Francisco, big in our bit of south Devon where the pedalos float and coach companies still had Magical Mystery Tours up on the moors.

Diane's bleeding again and crying and I've phoned for an ambulance. It wasn't always like this. In days gone by, The Cars were playing 'Good Times Roll' while we're tooting strong speed and drinking chilled white wine, smoking Marlboro Red and laughing; we're laughing and we've got money and more money, we've got more drugs and each other. We've got it all.

Right now, life was like a cliff railway car descending with no brakes. It was all fucked up, gone ugly with words and gestures and vicious actions involving sexual jealousy, barbiturates, theft, and violence. There was a bucket with blood, the sort of bucket you'd do your hand-washing in. I remember the blood, pouring it down the toilet. I thought there were bits, I can't be sure, but that memory has always haunted me. Everything was broken. We'd tried fixing things, but it was all unravelling. A doctor had visited the day before and prescribed my girlfriend Pethidine, a drug for childbirth pains. She'd been bleeding and now she'd miscarried. She was sick, I was on bail, and it was all getting worse. I called the ambulance. The paramedic asked me if there was any medication to take with her to the hospital. I said no.

For some reason, I was wearing a suit. I can't remember what I'd been up to earlier, but I had a suit on. Geraldo the moustachioed, quiffed Mexican on his American talk show would say, "It's not how you feel, it is how you look". I went over to Penny's to find Jimmy – he'd got a private doctor in London and I knew he'd have some amps of Physeptone and maybe some Ritalin. Jimmy had been out but didn't have keys to get back into Penny's where he'd stashed some drugs under the floorboards in the bathroom. Her building had scaffolding at the front, so I climbed up, got in through a bedroom room window, and unlocked the front door to let Jimmy in. Jimmy had been in a serious car accident a couple of years before – head injury, his balance fucked ever since. I scored the amps, shot them up, smoked, talked bollocks, and left. There was never any deep conversation between us.

A year previous to this Diane had had an abortion and it was arranged for a local taxi driver called Lawrence to take her to and from the clinic. He turned up inappropriately in a long, black Ford limousine. I can imagine her sitting alone in that car, an awful disconnect. I wasn't even there when she left. I bought her a dress as a pathetic form of compensation. Sometime later a girl in a laundrette near Pretty Park, Chelston, complimented her on it. This girl had sold it to me in Come West, a large store of independent traders near the harbour. I'd asked her to try it on, as she was the same size.

Lawrence was a bit of a mystery. He lived with his sister, talked in a whiney, clipped tone, dyed his eyebrows, and wore snide Liberty print cravats. He could've been a bogus major from a monotone Jonathon Meades narrative. He was a little bit sinister, but he always did us a deal. The number plate on one of his taxis included the letters DFC: he told me he was a holder of the Distinguished Flying Cross. I was sceptical. When he told you anything, he uttered the words like it was a secret, a confidence, a whiney whisper. Lawrence was a Poodle Faker if ever there was one, cultivating friendships with older women basically for reward. Afternoon teas and long drives up to the moors in his big and bouncy Vauxhall Cresta provided a platform for his performance, mesmerising the vulnerable and boring the more clued-up.

Occasionally, he'd sell me a few portables: silver coasters, picture frames, the odd bit of jewellery. They could have been trophies. He did eventually ensnare and marry a woman, moving to a small apartment in fashionable Wellswood. The word got out she wasn't the touch he thought she was. I did see him out shopping in the village as a married man, carrying a basket. He looked defeated, no hair dye or cravat – the out of control bushy eyebrow look: not a good one.

I eventually wander back to the flat alone, slightly removed, the anxiety dampened by the drugs. Later, there will be more drugs. I rub a 5/8 needle on a mirror to sharpen it and filter the chalk out of the Pethidine pills through a torn cigarette filter. The bed needs changing, and I put the sheets in a bucket to soak. I visit her in hospital the following day knowing it is all over but neither of us have the energy to go anywhere, so we'll stick together until we're torn apart. She will fuck around while I'm locked up and then we'll get back together and it'll happen again and again like a couple of pound shop Burton and Taylors, until finally coming to an end sometime in 1991.

I was an absolute bastard on a number of occasions. I'd get really jealous around her previous relationships, my own echo chamber of emptiness and too much time on my hands. I'd try and make sense of my behaviour and attitudes but for the most part I regret it ever occurred. I attempted pitiably to present an emotional response, a justification beyond my own capabilities, through the words of other people's songs, dipping into that deep well of lyrics enabling co-dependency. *Love and Affection* by Joan Armatrading was a prime example. We had gone into the local record shop and I wanted to buy Carole King's *Tapestry* album, but it was out of stock.

I tainted something that started off quite innocently and wore her down with my own disappointments. I had a book of Walter De La Mare's poetry, and she made me a beautiful tasselled, embroidered bookmark. Over the years, Di also knitted me jumpers and skilfully made her own clothes. I was too distracted to see the exquisiteness in the fine lining of the skirts or the cut of the leopard print jacket she fashioned. I knew the price of scrap silver, drugs, and the obvious collectables, but it was all about what I didn't have, not what I had. Diane was talented, there is no doubt about it, and I was too egocentric to see this, with my insecurities and relentless fuck-ups. I wish I could go back to the morning when she woke up laughing; start from that point out.

When I wasn't around, she wanted someone to love her and she made some questionable choices. Over the years, she changed and during an absence some charmer introduced her to chasing smack: the doll within the doll. I felt responsible for that and, when we got back together, the past came with us during screaming drunken nights of near car crashes and pavement dramas. I'd read Roger McGough's poem to her 'A Lot of Water has Flown under your Bridge', spoiling it by stressing the last-but-one verse. In many ways, we were a bad influence on each other and what didn't help was the fact her doctor had been prescribing her Valium since she was 16. At the time, there was still the Elvis mentality of prescription drugs being acceptable. I tore into her doctor's surgery once and had a go at him like a self-righteous fool.

I went to Battersea mid-August 1978 with my mum to see my granddad in his little widower's studio bungalow. I left Mum with her dad and popped over to see Johnny, my late Uncle Charlie's son, at Ethelburga Estate near Chelsea Bridge. Johnny and I went to The Cat's Whiskers in Streatham with a couple of girls he knew and then onto an all-night card game in Wandsworth at a low-rise council block. I'd rung home – Torquay 36562 – and asked Diane to collect some money from my pal Ali, who was a bass guitarist in the show band at the Paignton Festival Theatre. Ali and I had gone to school together and he'd sold a couple of early Elvis Presley albums on my behalf to the comedian Freddie Starr, who was playing at the theatre. I told her to buy a train ticket and meet me in London. I then left Johnny's and went back over to see my mum and the rest of the family. Mum suggested I phone Joe Grant, a pal of Dad's, who ran a nightclub in the West End. Joe tells me to get a minicab over the river and up West to Albemarle Street.

The club was in a basement, with a stage along the back wall, the ladies' and gents' toilets either side, and a small bar to the right of the entrance. Joe asked after my dad. I'd met Joe some years before in the Carlton Club and I knew he was someone you did not take liberties with. He asked me what I was up to and I explained that my girlfriend was coming up from Devon on the milk train, arriving at Paddington just before 5 a.m. Joe then introduced me to Tiny, who was huge with hands like plates. Tiny had been a butcher in Barnstable; I don't know how he met Joe, but he was now his sidekick. He told him to keep an eye on me and sent us off into the West End.

We went to a club called The Rockingham, where a doorman called Billy Keen introduced himself as a pal of my dad's and asked me to extend his regards. Tiny chatted and I took it all in, being extremely polite when spoken to. I'd been around the West End before but very much on the outside looking in. Now, I felt so much more part of it – it was like an acceptance.

We go back to the club. Joe has a manager who doubles as a singer – the West End ambience and the *tout ensemble* colludes in a convincing Frank Sinatra. The wine tasted like cherry cola and the champagne ginger ale, but I wasn't the one buying it. Joe arranges for Tiny to drive me to Paddington to collect Diane. The car was a Citroen Safari and we stopped at an all-night shop where I bought some drink. We drove straight down onto the platform where the mail vans used to go and Tiny sat against the bonnet while I looked out for her getting off the train. Good times. We stayed in Joe's *pied-à-terre* near Clapham Junction. There was a jukebox in the front room. Joe mentioned he'd been burgled some months previously and added, "Let the fuckers try getting that out the window".

CHANCERS

I was still half-cut from the night before – certainly nothing new there – cusping hyperactive with a window to a possible depressive episode. The challenge would be to obtain some form of further mood-altering chemical before the early afternoon decline. A cold, bright, low winter sun, freezing in the shadows and crisp at best in the glare. I'm in a phone box, on the same phone I called Johnson Brothers of Birmingham for silver prices a week previous. I'm now ringing a second-hand furniture dealer I know, regarding the contents of Barbara's late parents' front room. My cigarette clamped fingers spin five numbers as the ash drops onto the chrome dial. Come the pips, I push the 10 pence piece in the slot, hear the whirr, then connection. "Rowley?" I say, leaning into the whiff of the receiver.

"Rowley speaking". I always think of Timothy Spall's character in the comedy-drama *Auf Wiedersehen Pet* when I recall Rowley with his easy-going Brummie accent. "Alright Rowley, Gerry here – remember bric-a-brac tea chests, Wellswood garage – the lock-up?"

"Yeah – got you".

"You interested in some dark wood furniture? I'd say it's '30s going on utility – sideboard, drop-leaf table and chairs with leather seats, mostly front room furniture".

"Yeah, might be, where are you?"

There were also a matching pair of Edwardian bedside cabinets that historically would have concealed a potty – punters paint them white, they always sell. Rowley had bought pieces from me before; it was usually the sort of stuff I couldn't be bothered putting through auction, items popular with dealers, good for filling containers for export to the States, not really antique but old and interesting enough.

"Ellacombe Church Road opposite the phone box, number eight black front door – what time you looking at?"

"Right, it's nearly half 10 now. I'll get Ray to come over – he's on a job. Say 12-ish? He'll give you a price".

"That's good – thanks, Rowley".

"Cheers, Gerry".

The phone box door snaps back on its leather-retaining strap. I wondered who made them with the thick livid stitching? Was it prisoners? Maybe the same inmates who sewed mailbags with so many blanket stitches to the inch, and machine-treadled National Coal Board donkey jackets? I know about these things. I can still smell the ammonia from the piss-pot in the cell. "Seventy-eight on the fours, sir," barked the screw from the control box in the crow's foot with a view down all of the wings. The 'residents' counted in for the night. The finger-breaking steel-barred door clang and jaunty key jangle. I was the education orderly; a favourite of Major Luscombe who took the Current Affairs class. While under the same roof, I recognized I moved in a small and civilized circle of education officers and teachers with the added privilege of a single cell and a light I could turn off.

Passing thoughts containing a combination of caution and

consequential detail follow me across the road and up four steps
to the front door left on the snib. My fellow pirate Regan is in the
front room trying to sew a Berlebeck brown leather button onto
his coat and Barry Manilow's record *Can't Smile Without You* is
playing on the stereogram.

"What did Rowley say?"

"He's sending Ray up 'bout 12".

We polish off a bottle of Natural Dry cider, clear the table, and
empty everything out of the drawers. Regan's wearing his brown
fake-fur-collared corduroy jacket, now with a full complement of
matching buttons, looking a tad like Clark Gable, same bad skin
and hairstyle. We're in a truly depressing room – the whole place
has something of the austere 1940s. The once bright, illuminated
fascia of the Decca radiogram is now fading but is still probably
the youngest item in the room apart from the plunderers. The items
have been waiting in nervous anticipation since the death of their
original possessors, people restricted by budget and taste. Barbara's
parents had lovingly chosen, cherished, and polished these items
over the years for the only child to neglect, tarnish and, at worse,
abuse their brittle veneers. They knew this day was coming and it
could have been a lot worse, it could've been a fire; their legacy now
to be no more than ghostly indentations on the thin, worn hessian-
backed carpet with no underlay. Aesthetically punished before the
war and, through use of utility furniture, aesthetically punished
after the Second World War. In the 1970s and '80s, there were
certain small items of furniture frequently found in charity shops:
ugly magazine racks of pressed copper with embossed galleons and
brown hexagonal plywood occasional tables. Was there any excuse
for this relentless bad taste? I considered this act one of liberation;

the mostly heavy brown furniture was being given another chance, a new lease of life.

The 1980s: yuppies, *Tiswas*, wine bars, the miners, and Elton John is collecting Art Deco. I want Art Deco too, but I'd settle for some Nouveau Emile Galle. I want Elton's piano and earrings. I remember watching Liberace on TV one night with my mum. He was playing Las Vegas, he pointed with a jewel-encrusted finger at the grand piano and gushingly stated, "There are only two of these pianos in the world and the other is in my conservatory at home". I wanted that piano more than Elton John's and I wanted an obscene heft of Georgian Paul Storr silver; I want bundles of high denomination cash thick enough to choke a donkey. I want to feel better about myself, I want to be in a constant state of bliss, running like a dynamo hum on drugs that make the banal bearable, that make my empty, pathetic existence bearable. I don't really want to be here doing this but I'm too lazy to explore other options today and it does have elements of a jolly jape. Fucking roll on 12 o'clock – he'd better want this shit.

This whole scenario began with Barbara's boyfriend Basil, a Cornish ex-trawlerman who borrowed money from Regan and made no attempt whatsoever to pay it back. Basil, the eternal bachelor, man child, living at his parent's house in an attractive part of Torquay, banished to a converted utility room under their house proper. Barbara would have supported him in this decision to renege, relishing a bit of conflict. It wasn't a great deal of money, but it was a liberty and certainly if it had been the other way around Basil would have been relentless in his quest for repayment. Basil was an extremely annoying individual; he could be a real nuisance. When drunk he would wave his hands up and down and intone, "*Ooh ooh*," at the beginning and end of sentences. There was a sing-songy Cornish burr to his accent when he was sober and then a low register drone with the *ooh oohs* when drunk. He made me want to hit him. I didn't of course, but I just wanted it to stop – that's how bad it could get. Basil always wore a black-peaked cap, had bad posture, and walked with a bit of a sway as if he was permanently on a yacht in a choppy harbour. He had a penchant for Bing Crosby and military bands, whereas Barbara adored Tony Bennett and Barry Manilow.

Barbara was in her early forties, petite and pleasingly rounded; she moved in an exaggeratedly delicate fashion. Her hair was a bob style, dyed black, she always wore a little too much kohl eye make-up and her skirts were extremely short. Tabu perfume, stale booze, and sweat was the familiar waft. Her accent would vary depending on her alcohol intake: late Friday afternoons it was usually Midlands aspiring posh but as her drinking progressed, she would get leery and start channelling Mancunian film noir. Eventually, it would become flat-out viperfish. Slurring and facially-contorted, she would end up attacking Basil's many flaws, turning on anyone who defended him.

I would sometimes use their bathroom to shoot speed. There is something cleansing about using in a bathroom – all the evidence can be flushed away, a clean start as you exit. I'd make my entrance onto the landing and clasp the bannisters like Il Duce as the blood soared through restricted capillaries, sparking up a snout as I descended into the chaos. Occasionally, there would be a card game, usually twenty-one, which would typically end in absolute mayhem, the scarred and ring-stained table tipping over, ashtrays thudding onto the scuffed and sticky red-and-black patterned carpet. A clearing up, another drink, fade to dawn – waking up awkwardly on the settee in the house of neglect. Although Barbara had inherited it, she didn't live there. She spent most of her time at a fifth floor 1960s apartment in Paignton; it had its own balcony and overlooked the Festival Theatre on the seafront. I don't think Basil was welcome there. I did stay there once; it was almost a 'behind the scenes' experience.

The first time I'd ever visited this neglected drinking den was at the invitation of Regan. He'd told Barbara I knew something about antiques – she had some china and wanted someone to have a look at it. It was all reasonably civilized on a scale of what my life was like then. Of course, heavy drinking was par for the course. Clearly, all the choice pieces had been sold off and this was just the back-of-the-sideboard oddments. In the green baize cutlery drawer, there were a few bone-handled button hooks, fuses, and a corkscrew. It was like picking over the carcass of a home. There was always an element of voyeurism in this sort of carry-on and I did enjoy it. You knew this wasn't ever going to be about business, it was about loneliness and drinking and slinking off until the next time, the next session, starting by making excuses as to what occurred previously.

Barbara did hold down a responsible job working in a secretarial capacity for the local council. She had self-published a couple of romantic novels that I suspect could've been construed as love letters, a script of 'what might have been'. Basil was in his late forties and his main claim to fame had been stealing a trawler some years previously and making for France. I think he got 12 months in prison. Maybe there was more to him than I knew. It was a curious relationship; I never witnessed any display of intimacy between them.

Whenever Regan and I went to Barbara's, Basil, 'the man of the house', would invariably answer the door with, "Ooh, here's trouble".

You would hear Barbara's melodious tones from the front room, "Don't be rude dear, invite them in". And there we would be, sitting in front of 'Miss' on the settee, grinning like two naughty schoolboys. "Would you like a drink? We've got cider or sherry". We'd always request cider in a polite and respectful manner as if partaking of a fine dining experience. As the dirty glasses were handed to us, she'd enquire: "And what have you boys been up to today?"

Before we could answer, Basil would go into fast hand-flapping mode, "Ooh, don't ask them that, you don't want to know – keep your own counsel".

Barbara would then turn on him like Elizabeth Taylor's character in the movie *Who's Afraid of Virginia Woolf?*, "Stop it Basil, stop saying silly things, we're trying to have a conversation!"

She actually enjoyed our company, fluttering her false eyelashes and making pre-Instagram pouts. In a manner of speaking, we did pay our way. Regan would make a point of lighting her cigarettes and I would give her meaningful looks. Once, when an ambulance screamed up the road, she caught my eye and cooingly whispered to Basil, "Ahh, Basil, here comes your taxi". The days of three channels on the television; it was more about people, not watching them but being with them, and the richness of the characters we met. Some were dangerous, some were hilarious, some were both. Scenarios by way of Bruce Robinson, the writer of *Withnail and I*, channelling Joe Orton.

Ray turned up at the appointed time. Some weeks previously, I'd sold him some blanket chests and Neff cooker hobs from some high-end holiday apartments that were being refurbished. It was evident they weren't mine to sell; we were laughing about it as we loaded it up – he didn't care, it was down to me if it came on top and I certainly didn't give a fuck. And now here we were coming to an agreement over a load of tat that would enable me to enhance my mood throughout the day, Regan to keep drinking and get a mixed doner with aubergine sauce from Ali the Turk later that night. A friend of mine once did some building work for Ali and when he inquired if Ali had planning permission Ali retorted, "You have my permission – get on with it".

There were a number of 45 singles with no sleeves in a wire-framed record rack with its little red plastic feet sitting on the radiogram. I selected Chris Montez, on the London label, singing 'Let's Dance', as we readily assisted Ray moving the furniture out the front room, down the steps, and into the back of a white Luton-back Transit.

DISTRACTION NUMBER SIX

Outside storm Ciara is raging by Whitechapel standards and I'm watching *Lost in Translation* on Netflix. Even though it's early February, the buds are growing on the tree outside my kitchen window. I watch the tree flex and sway. I couldn't bear anything to happen to this tree – trees are at a premium around here. There is a magpie nest on the top. I don't like their raspy chatter, I prefer the tweet and chirp of small, flitting birds. A ginger tom cat with a big-scarred head is always climbing the tree trying to get at the magpies. The cat has no fear and will try and barge his way onto the landings when the main door is opened. I always say to him, "Alright, mate?", but I've never stroked him.

A friend of mine stayed at the flat last night. She practices hypnotherapy in Edinburgh and Glasgow and was in London attending a workshop in High Holborn. As a gift she left me a book: *Japanese Wisdom for a Perfectly Imperfect World*. I'm always wary of counsellor types – anyone on a mission really – 'I was a bastard and then I found Jesus'. An element of 'I drive a car therefore I'm a mechanic'. When I consider some of my more balanced friends I realize they've usually done some work on themselves, they've had counselling or therapy. My excuse is purely lack of finances. I don't know what I'm frightened of losing, apart from money of course.

Politicians are like Asda cheeses – they come in different colours but all taste the same. London should be another country. In London, institutions will happily offer tens of thousands of pounds for an hour-long lecture yet in the name of "economic rationality" refuse to pay their cleaners a living wage. Jim Royle barks, "Churchill, my arse," at the Bullingham pretender. People with integrity don't tell lies and people with ability don't hide in fridges. Even truly wicked leaders had boltholes with names like the 'Wolf's Lair', while the philandering liar can only manage a Kent country house monikered 'Chevening'. Sounds more like a Richmond poodle parlour. My friend Kenneth remarked that most politicians are like actors thrown on stage who've forgotten their lines. In an age of performative cruelty, kindness is punk as fuck. Be punk as fuck.

There is an ill wind blowing.

A TUMBLE OF MEMORY FROM
THE TURRET TO BREAKFAST TV

MUM DIED ON 10th February 1983. She was 49 years old. At the time, I was living in the turret of a big old Victorian pile in Torquay. A narrow staircase led from a galley kitchen to my cold square bedroom from where I had a view of the catholic school I'd once attended. I had no happy memories of that school. I'd lived in a pub in this area as a child and memories were literally around the corner.

I was talking on the wall-mounted beige and black communal telephone in the hallway downstairs when my dad pulled up outside in a white Ford Cortina. There was a cold, bright sun and I could see the car park through the open door. As he got out of the motor, he shouted at me, "Get off the phone – get off the fucking phone. Your mother's dead". I'm sure the time was about 11.30 and my brother Ian was with him. Ian stayed in the car, providing the mood by proxy for the old man. I don't recall much of the following conversation, probably a mention of arrangements. I felt guilty, somehow complicit. That's the nature of addiction – it's all about you. Immediately, I wanted to change the way I felt and that was my plan – to get off my head from the minute I was told. The phone call was connected to scoring, so really it was business as usual with a heavy dose of justified self-pity.

Diagnosed with dementia, Mum had been ambulanced from an Exeter hospital to a Victorian villa in Torquay that had been converted into a nursing home. She would have been driven down roads she had once cruised with scarfed-hair and an Embassy cigarette on her honeymoon in 1955. This nursing home was located on one of Torquay's seven hills. I imagine there would have been small talk between the driver and his mate – just another job, just another day. They wouldn't know of the fabulous bar mitzvah Mum attended at the Dorchester Hotel in London when she worked for Morgan Crucible, or the visits to Freddie Mills' Nite Spot. I only hope they treated her with respect as she was conveyed between destinations of limbo.

The last time I saw Mum alive was on a Sunday, after the pubs but before *Songs of Praise*. I had tucked a bottle of cider behind one of the wooden metal-hinged studded double doors at the entrance of the nursing home. We met on a broad ornate wooden staircase in a galleried entrance hall that could've been painted by Dorothea Tanning, the American surrealist. Mum didn't recognize me, looking around and not at me. She was so frail, and I noticed she had a slight overbite giving her a look of constant inquiry. Being brought up during sweet rationing she had all her own teeth. Why did she have to contend with so much suffering? The rings rattled on her fingers. Those rings would disappear, the same as Dad's wallet when he was in a nursing home in Devons Road, 2007. Is it a trade-off with institutional care, the low wages and long hours? It is not a criticism, it's life experience. My own self-worth prevented me from taking Mum's rings with me, knowing I'd sell them for drugs.

Mum was small, bird-like, and I was just awkward. Everything was out of scale. We were just standing, lost in this dark, murmuring building and I was trying to get through to her, looking for a glimmer, a connection. It felt as if I had been presented with evidence of her condition and, now that I'd witnessed the void, there was no need to return. We didn't even sit down together – we just stood there. That was the last time I kissed her. There was nothing in it for me and I couldn't just be around and watch on a daily basis something I knew nothing about. I didn't have the staying power, the selfless dedication.

1965, Labenne, South West France. Miles of unspoilt beaches and Dad making camps out of driftwood. A local Orangina-like drink dispensed from a hinged porcelain and rubber-stoppered bottle. Mum in a bikini with frills and my baby brother a couple of years old. In Biarritz, a freak wave threw Mum against some rocks. Dad dragged her out and I apparently grabbed my brother. Did it happen like that? On the drive back to Le Touquet I always remember tomatoes with a mayonnaise potato salad and chives. The head gasket was to blow on the silver-grey Vauxhall Victor estate near Paris. Eventually, we arrived back at the airport and drove up the ramp into the nose of the aircraft car transporter *Silver City*. It was a loud shuddering flight back to Lydd in Kent.

Everybody wants to say how much they loved their mother. I try, but the distance, circumstances, and memories are deep with sadness, longing, and the bitter truth that we didn't know each other that well.

Everything was so fragmented. Breakfast TV had just started airing. A weatherman later exposed as a sex offender leapt about all over a UK-shaped pontoon on a redundant Manchester ship canal. His stupid jumpers were the highpoint of some sad bastard's morning together with the exaggerated high energy of the Green Goddess and Mr. Motivator. I used to watch it with the volume turned down, doing speed and listening to the UK Subs and Blondie. Janet Street Porter was representative of this time, her 'Yoof TV' a total construct. But I didn't know any better then and everybody was buying it. Who was I to throw stones from my cold turret window?

THE FLIP

CANNON AND BALL, Little and Large – hardly comparable to Morecambe and Wise or the Two Ronnies. The creep of shit simulacra. A Boston square-back haircut, still cool, copied from an Italianate model on the wall of Paul the Continental Hairdresser. "Give my regards to your father, Gerry. You being a good boy?" Doctor's bags – if all else fails, hit the doctor's bags. Occasionally getting the 'good stuff': Diamorphine ampoules, but more often than not it was Valium amps – blood clotting in the works as you render yourself unconscious. Getting hold of Heminevrin, as used in treating and preventing symptoms of acute alcohol withdrawal; extracting the liquid contents with a fuck-off green needle... Get it in there! Then, there were the care assistants in the nursing homes, with names like Stella and Tracey, raiding the hardly accountable drug trolleys. Temgesic, Diconal, morphine sulphate, to name the popular choices of the day. It's not what I want but it's better than nothing and it's winter and the wheel spins round in the coin-fed electric meter while I feel every bit a failure. It'll take me a lifetime to realise most success is based on turning up every day.

The reality outside the reality, the naughty loop. I was operating in the naughty loop and Regan would tap up his stepmother for a painting she never 'used', kept in the attic. One of the Cornish school of painters, Newlyn, St Ives or Falmouth, circa 1930. We'd find out it was in a naïve style and get high hundreds for it. I was running out of energy, spending mornings in the company of heavily made-up older women who cleaned their rings in gin and ran antique emporiums. Due to the Bunker Hunt brothers trying to corner the silver market, precious metal prices were good. This was a time of cutlery and coins. Florins, half-crowns, and sixpences pre-1947 and 1919, antique shops, vitrine glass cases, lower end, fusty not beeswax, but the cash was high denomination notes and the ink stank lovely. The auctions and vans with their back doors open, promising treasure. Cutting your hands on the rusty bodywork of old Transits, feeding sieved radiators with raw egg as a 'temporary' measure. The furs; Canadian silver fox, mink, Persian lamb. The spiel would be along the lines of, "It's a bit greasy – needs a clean. Nah, to me it's worth 180. Yeah, yeah, the valuation might well be 1,200. Take it or leave it. Or, you could insure it for that and burn the fucking house down". Silk lining on the stoles, twisted silk cords for the bite of the clasp.

All of this was reduced to some powder in a spoon, not forgetting the craic in the pub. Those rainy afternoon lock-ins: the cloying smell of Calor gas fires, and an AMI jukebox quietly plays, sans bass, Roy Orbison's 'It's Over' as the jokes and scenarios flowed. Spoofing with Hungarian George and then in the taxi to score, swishing away in a quarter-to-six half-light bouncing off wet oily roads as the driver, who knows the landlord, asks if it's been a good session. Loud tipping, goodbyes, and sparking up on the move, swaggering to the front door and then cooking up below the eye-level grill in a lino-floored, bright, single bulb kitchen. My dealer kisses me, my 'I can get' as she hits me up – pulling that rose in – then flushing the works and Lee Scratch Perry spins 'I Chase the Devil' in the front room. What more do you want?

Flip that switch. I watched an interview once with Mick Jagger; he was asked about the popularity of the Stones and whether he thought it would endure. Jagger replied that fans wouldn't all stop coming to concerts overnight – it would be a gradual drift, if it were to happen at all. The naughty loop escalated incrementally, everything tuned in differently, and Regan commented, "If I was going to get into this shit, I'd make sure I had a basement full of it". The only thing that really counted now was how much I had in my pocket and could I score. The stakes get higher; it was all getting more serious but, just like swearing on the bible years before, nothing changed. Overdoses don't count when you come around and all the bollocks about waking up in hospital. Walking away from car crashes, just missing serious shit. So, what. So, fucking, what! The only thing that really counts now is how much you've got in your pocket – can you get, can you score? As Turner said in the film *Performance*, "The only performance that makes it, that makes it all the way, is the one that achieves madness".

On reflection, the people I met through buying and selling were a lot more interesting than the drug culture. Most addicts were fucking boring – including myself come the end.

BAGGAGE

WHEN I MET Diane, she lived at home and worked as a bookkeeper for a town centre optician. Her room with its single bed and Bowie posters was directly above the front door porch roof. She told me she'd stuff her teddy bear between her bedroom wall and headboard when having sex, boyfriends exiting via the porch roof. Her father had been a career soldier, a recipient of the British Empire Medal, and a witness at Bikini Atoll. For her eighteenth birthday, he bought her a burgundy imitation leather suitcase with locks and buckle brass straps. Shortly after this birthday present of unsubtle encouragement, she moved in with me. I would borrow her suitcase and in my possession it was to see active service in Europe and the Asian sub-continent, making its entrance and exit in Madrid, Brussels, pre-Mumbai Bombay and Delhi, sweeping through Paris, London, and then back on the top of a heavy, inlaid Edwardian wardrobe in Torquay.

Smoking and drinking on a 747 between Brussels and Mumbai with a German import -export agent based in Singapore, his Philippine wife constantly delving into her vanity case then adjusting her make-up. The German actually said to me, "You should go to the Philippines and get yourself a wife." His wife smiled at me, complicit in this conceit. I wonder how I managed to keep the banter up for thousands of miles. But then deceit came easily.

Chloe perfume purchased from the duty free in a Lalique bottle. My childish penchant for lozenge-shaped Pez sweets and their whacky dispensers.

Daydreams of wood-ribbed and heavy leather cabin trunks with their fading and peeling glued labels from exotic destinations such as Monte Carlo and Copacabana. The age of the wireless, puttees, chits, and verandas, when Cadillac-fronted Bakelite radios could be tuned into Prague, Hilversum, Berlin, and Marseilles. A BBC television series starring Trevor Howard and Celia Johnson as ex-pats remaining, seeing their days out in the cool hill stations of Shimla. Flying boats with a choice of a dozen different wines and the first air hostesses were qualified nurses.

I could justify my criminality by comparing the corporate opioid pollution of whole communities with OxyContin, pumping this poison out through the pill mills of the Midwest in the United States. I was stitching the plastic-sealed powder into the panels of my little briefcase while these corporations were limbering up to start wreaking havoc. They unleashed a commission-based epidemic surpassing the devastation of early '80s crack cocaine in deprived communities. All this endorsed by many trusted doctors, who prescribed this gear while telling people the pills weren't addictive. But then it's not about them, it's about me. Wanting to live like a pop star who couldn't read music or play an instrument.

NICKED

"I WARNED YOU son, I told you this would happen – this is what happens when you hang around with cunts".

I recognized a similar phrase in the Big Lebowski some years later: "Do you see, Donny, do you see? This is what happens when you fuck someone up the ass you don't know".

"Look, I know, I'm sorry…"

"It's a bit fucking late for that now – it breaks my heart to see you here. I didn't bring you up like this". Dad discreetly passed me a quarter bottle of Smirnoff, his broad shoulders screening the Georgian wire glass door behind him. I ducked down and necked it in three swallows, palming the bottle back to him. It was the most natural thing in the world.

"You've got to knock this bollocks on the head – look at the trouble you're in".

"I know – I know!". But I know fuck all and if I got out now, if I got bail – I'd score straight away. I couldn't feel any further than that. I could smell cigars on the old man, he probably had a session at lunchtime; it was about 3.30 p.m., pubs closed at half two.

"I've left some cigarettes for you". Never fags, always cigarettes.

I mumbled, "Thanks, Dad," and started to feel a warm glow, watering my eyes, the spirit taking the edge off – momentarily. I picked at the corner of the table; the top covering is like lino with sacking weave underneath – institutions.

Dad stretched his hand across his forehead and massaged his temples, washing his face with his hand and looking at me, slightly tilted, head sideways. "Joe," he hesitates, "My pals in London have nothing to do with drugs, it's a mug's game. I don't know how you can do it to yourself, fucking needles. Christ, just get off this shit, use this time, it'll be alright."

I knew Joe. He'd run clubs in London: Albemarle Street near Piccadilly, opposite Browns Hotel and latterly Rupert Street. Joe placed adverts in men's magazines, offering to collect people from their hotel in a chauffeur driven car and show them the delights of Soho, especially his club *L'Apache*. Joe likes his weed and is partial to coke but it wouldn't be clever saying this now. A number of Dad's pals are functioning alcoholics, the difference is they don't get nicked or at least he doesn't mention it if they do. Joe told me years later about one of his smuggling excursions from North Africa to Spain with a case of cannabis. One of Joe's pals was involved in the kidnapping of the train robber Ronnie Biggs. Not cool.

Dad was very old school. Some of his contemporaries from his boxing days were doing time for robbery. This was the age of *The Sweeney* TV show and smashed Jags, sawn-off shotguns, flares, and stocking-headed blaggers. In the 1950s, Dad had lost a significant fight, over 12 rounds, to Peter Waterman, the older brother of Denis Waterman who starred in *The Sweeney*. Dad lost on points – it was a contentious issue and it rankled. One time he asked Beryl at the *Thomas a Becket* when so-and-so might be in and he was told they're doing 15 years. Beryl Cameron-Gibbons ran the *Becket* on the Old Kent Road for years until 1983. Then she was

Europe's only female boxing promoter. The old man used to train there and I remember him taking me in when we'd go back up to The Smoke in the 1970s. Tough guys and lock-ins and playing a game on the bar that involved holding a handle with an insulated loop and guiding, with a steady hand, the loop over an undulating wire suspended between two posts. If you touched the wire, a loud bell would go off.

Many of Dad's acquaintances got up to all sorts of malarkey. During the late 1970s, illegal bare-knuckle fights were an earner for some of the 1950s fighters. Colluding minicab drivers would set up Arabs with casino-stuffed clutch bags so that ex-fighters could come out of the shadows and deck them with one punch. Nothing personal, just business. It wasn't all criminality, but I remember the network of acquaintances Dad retained throughout his life, guys he'd met boxing and through his National Service. Unfortunately, I was surrounded by people who'd rat on me as soon as look at me to save themselves. This certainly included my girlfriend and my own brother. It's awful to admit but it was true. It said a lot about me as well.

There is a scene in the film *Quadrophenia* where two boxers are sparring in a gym. The sharp-suited tough guy John Bindon sorts Phil Daniels out for French Blues (speed). As he sends Daniels off to score, he turns to a colleague and says, "Pill head... tosser." Bindon always reminded me of my Uncle Charlie, Johnny's father. He was flash, a right smoothie, but an utter nightmare to his wife. The scene resonated for me, the controlling and confident guys in the gym and me feeling like an absolute waster and weak. I was under no illusion. I'd got caught and in this brutal despair, saturated with self-pity, I was recalling good times with my dad. I longed to be sitting outside a pub on the cream passenger seat of a red convertible Buick eating crisps and drinking coke waiting for Dad and Charlie. I'd gone from narcotic bliss, swanning around Madrid in my Lois jeans and silk jacket, to a stale piss-stinking cell with Izal toilet paper and grim looks from the family solicitor. All this was well outside his normal remit and I was entering the realm of the hopeless and truly miserable.

I'm skint, all the dough is done, and the prosecution is objecting to bail, "Due to the nature and gravity of the offence and because he has contacts in Europe and the Indian subcontinent..." I'm standing in the dock wearing a classic grey, double-breasted Dior suit with my reptile-skin Grensons, without even the fucking bus fare to Newton Abbot, five miles up the road.

I was in a cell at the back of the courthouse with a guy named Eric, who was shouting for a screw, "Boss, let us use the khazi, I've got a turtle's head here." Eric had been a mechanic in Liverpool, who'd been tempted by what appeared easy money and now he was bursting for a tom-tit in a south coast magistrates court holding cell.

Six months prior to this courthouse scene, I'd become involved with a motley crew, consisting of a morbidly obese drayman and a white Y-fronts wearing property developer, who aspired to be a DJ. The Y-fronts wearer had confided in me, during a trip to Newport to collect a passport, that white pants provided an early indication of any weeping sexually transmitted disease. Apparently, he was routinely unfaithful to his hairdressing wife. I felt really uneasy about this sort of shit and as we were smoking weed, I was getting the horrors. Years later, his wife divorced him, and he took up with an Eastern European hostess type – trout pout and big ponytail.

Another character on their periphery was a pug-faced ex-chef who had something of the Mickey Rooney and could be a nasty piece of work. I suspected he'd had a really grim upbringing. He's long gone now but he was to spawn a family that featured in the television programme *Neighbours from Hell.*

Years before all this, prior to his obesity, I'd got together with the drayman's girlfriend, when she had said, "Kiss me," at some drunken party. I'd always felt uneasy about this, like I should've known better. I later found out the beer delivery boy had been quite happy sharing her with one of his friends. I always suspected him of robbing my parents' electric meter and later my brothers. It was about his level; he wasn't very bright. This was a man that kept all his depositions even though they were damning evidence of his dobbing his co-accused in. A few of my girlfriends were grammar schoolgirls and it did make me question the grammar school selection process. I made the grammar school stream of the catholic school, but I always considered this a consolation prize, like the *Tudor* to the *Rolex:* I would have preferred the *Rolex,* not the one made by the subsidiary. Around the time of my 11-plus, I don't even remember being at school; this was when mum was in hospital and my brother and I lived at different addresses from London to Plymouth and up to Scotland.

DISTRACTION NUMBER SEVEN

My hallway was painted a muted grey, a fashionably pastel shade.
There was something tame German army about it. On the wall,
immediately above the bedroom and front room doors, is a single
'Marilyn' – isolated from the *Diptych* – in a black frame. It was a
present from an ex-girlfriend named Francine, who once took me to
New York for a Jewish family wedding and brought this print back
from MOMA on a subsequent visit. There is a block of turquoise colour
to the right of Marilyn's neck where a shadow would be and for me
it stands out against the gold background. I decided to repaint the
hallway a duck-egg blue. While the 'Marilyn' turquoise is brighter,
it perfectly complements the new wall colour. On the front room
door, behind a Perspex cover, is a photographic self-portrait of Andy
Warhol, announcing his exhibition at Tate Modern, but it omits the
extended dates due to Covid-19.

New York City, late 1964: Dorothy Podber arrived at the Warhol
'Factory' on East 47th Street clad in black motorcycle leathers and
wearing white gloves. She was accompanied by a couple of friends
and her Great Dane, Carmen Miranda. After theatrically removing
her gloves, she pulled a small black gun out of her pocket and aimed it
at Warhol before turning to a stack of four paintings propped against
the wall and pulling the trigger, shooting Marilyn Monroe through

the head four times.

I have on occasion sat in Tate Modern looking at the *Marilyn Diptych* for a considerable amount of time, a sort of self-imposed screen test. I noticed the subtle differences, the painterly qualities of the left panel, familiar things, variations in hair and lips and the extreme fades from near-white to black on the right panel. I wondered who had just caught the bottom of the left-hand coloured canvas with a daub, a turquoise daub; was it Warhol or maybe Gerard Malanga, the poet who taught Warhol how to silkscreen print? I have noticed all these things before, but I never tire of them. Like listening to the Miles Davis album *Kind of Blue*, being aware of its genius inception, or when I used to smoke – the satisfaction of inhaling stubby American Marlboros, each one tasting as good as the last.

The *Marilyn Diptych* visually emotes an ecclesiastical Byzantine presence and whilst these are not the 'shot Marilyns' – also referred to as the 'Lifesavers', alluding to the candies similar to British Polo Fruits – this work does share the same geographical, edgy, and glamorous provenance of being created in the East 47th Street Factory, the two-hinged tablets in this case equal in size but differing in colour. The cinematic Technicolor film frames of this work flip to black-and-white; the black-and-white of classic Hollywood, shot on cameras freighted from warehouses in a cold New York City to the Californian sunshine.

Religious iconography has its roots in Warhol's childhood in Pittsburgh. His mother Julia, always a solid presence throughout his life, was a deeply religious woman and the boy Warhol would have been exposed to the interior of churches both in her company and later in life through commitment to his own faith. I once heard Will Self say on Question Time, "Politics is show business for ugly people."

I would counter: Churches are show business for poor people. Warhol grew up in an area where the main industries were coal and steel. He found respite within the sacred – attracted to the rich brocades, the ecclesiastical adornments of the priests, in sharp contrast to the anthracite grey and the soot-blackened environment of Pittsburgh.

April 1972: Bowie played live in Plymouth and my pal Martin drove me to the concert in his blue Mini, assuring my mum he'd look after me. Later in July, the same year, I watched Bowie sing 'Starman', this time in Torquay. I bought his album *The Rise and Fall of Ziggy Stardust and the Spiders from Mars* and the earlier album *Hunky Dory*. At my secondary modern school, there was a bearded art teacher, a Capri-driving, ageing Lothario who, it was rumoured, was shagging the domestic science teacher. Apparently, in his younger days, he'd drank with the writer William Burroughs in a bar in Tangier. He allowed us to bring our vinyl albums to class and play them while we worked. David Bowie's *Hunky Dory* has a track called 'Andy Warhol'. The art teacher brought in some magazines featuring Warhol's work and this was the first time I saw the 'Marilyns'.

I read in *New Musical Express* or somewhere that Warhol had covered his working space in silver foil – an idea he'd got from Billy Name, the Factory's official photographer and caretaker. Silver was the future, the space age. My bedroom ceiling was covered in silver foil and I painted a wall purple. I had an *International Times* annual with a silver foil cover. Teenage years are so significant. Summer holidays go on forever, the memories and inspirations fixing hard to the future. Bunking in to the local cinema underage – hitting the exit door at a right angle and springing it – and watching a double bill of *The Graduate* and *Midnight Cowboy* with its party scene of Warhol Superstars. I treasured my double album compilation of

Andy Warhol's Velvet Underground featuring Nico, the album cover artwork and inside gatefold sleeve featuring Warhol's *Coca-Cola* paintings.

The years roll on, the scratch static crackles amplifying. Bianca Jagger riding a white horse on her 30th birthday through Studio 54 in Manhattan. The club was to burn bright for 33 months until the IRS and narcs started sniffing around. Sex and death – celebrity and money. Warhol's Mick Jagger screen-prints – selling Jagger to Jagger. The bright Polaroid bulb flash instantly whiting out and eradicating time-telling lines and sags. There is quite a lot of documentation of Warhol and Mick together – a mutual admiration for an extremely skilful economy of cultural movement perhaps? Liza with a Zee, posing against a blank background after *Cabaret*. The effortless translation to canvas and eternal youth, Warhol sold America back to the Americans. Images to reflect the dysfunction of time, as if Warhol knew beauty couldn't last and all was becoming disposable. Old Smokey the electric chair, Elvis, Marilyn, Campbell's, Brillo, and more celebrity, new celebrity, create celebrity. Let's talk about Monroe as the great and the good are immortalized, some greater than others, such as Mohammad Ali.

The cultural commodification of the 1970 and '80s and the guest list of Studio 54, being swiped under a squeegee – skills that had taken a lifetime to refine, not forgetting the delegation and quiet collaboration. Seeing Warhol interviewed, the monosyllabic responses, the otherness. I'll be your mirror. The cold detachment of a voyeur – the clues are all there, the films without soundtrack – the Empire State waiting for the tip to light up and round to dawn. The hours of taped phone calls, the constant entourage of dysfunctional and marginalized individuals. "In the future, everyone will be famous for 15 minutes". A performative phrase, in itself a self-fulfilling prophecy. The magnificent 'Marilyns' with the off-register colours suggest an hallucinogenic experience – Haight-Ashbury, San Francisco. Be sure to wear a flower in your hair. But the Marilyns were created four to five years before the Merry Pranksters of Ken Kesey got on the bus, its destination reading 'Further', sharing their LSD sugar cubes. Warhol tuned the dial in on the zeitgeist before it happened.

The 1930-40s photographer Weegee – whose sobriquet derived from the 'Ouija' spirit board and his almost psychic ability to be where the action was – liked a big, boofing, cracking flash for the stabbings, shootings, and hookers. Andy Warhol just watched and considered. The Beatle John Lennon had once stated, "If there hadn't been Elvis, there wouldn't have been The Beatles". Consider R. Mutt's 'Fountain' – Duchamp's decision to select an everyday item and present it as art. Would there have been Warhol without Duchamp? Warhol anointed celebrity as object. He recognized just how loaded with cultural reference the famous and infamous can be. Marilyn had sung for a President. Watching a rerun of the *Elvis '68 Comeback Special*, I realized I'd seen his stance before – Warhol had swiped the pistol-toting King across a silkscreen in 1962. The chosen two holograms elevated to almost papal reverence in the 2017 film *Blade Runner 2049* are Marilyn Monroe and Elvis Presley. Warhol's ghostly hand – from celebrity to high culture.

The work never stops coming. *Songs for Drella* (Drella being Warhol's nickname, a composite on Dracula and Cinderella) is an insightful homage by Lou Reed and the Welsh musician John Cale. They eulogize his work ethic, taking a journey through his life so beautifully, so New York 'matter of factly' – with some brutal street

179

honesty.

There were three Factories. The first was on East 47th Street, Midtown Manhattan, where the 'Marilyns' were created. The smell of cordite from the shot Marilyns followed him to the next Factory in the Decker Building, Union Square West. Here Valerie Solanas waited for him, shot at him three times, and hit him once. The one bullet was to cause devastation and leave him in discomfort for the rest of his life. This was all due to a perceived slight, mental illness, and no clear lines of communication. The subject matter he had dealt with in his art practice segued into his life. Death was now real. The investment needed protecting from itself. "Making money is art and working is art and good business is the best art," said Warhol. The final Factory was more corporate, more business-orientated, with white, open spaces. The street never got through the door again.

One of Warhol's first ever exhibitions was a window display at Bonwit Teller, a large sophisticated retail store with an Art Nouveau style frontage, located on Fifth Avenue and 56th Street, New York City. Warhol was in good company; in 1939, Salvador Dali designed the window display featuring a bathtub lined with Persian lamb. In 1980, Donald Trump demolished the building. The limestone dancing women he'd previously said he would give to the Metropolitan Museum were destroyed. The Gotham City edifice that is now Trump Tower rose out of the rubble. I think Warhol would have appreciated the irony, in a presidential monosyllabic fashion.

I attended the Warhol biography book launch on 12th March 2020 in the Starr Cinema at Tate Modern. I was pleasantly surprised at how much I already knew about Warhol. I bought a copy of Blake Gopnik's 1,000-page book. He signed it for me and was the last person I shook hands with before lockdown.

DEAR JOHN

HOW DID THIS happen, how did I get here? How did I end up on a 56-seater coach like a bad trip *Magical Mystery Tour*, with 16 other accused? Fourteen months on remand. Mike, the Vidal Sassoon trained hairdresser from Blackpool, was to make a video for the police demonstrating how he defrauded the Post Office, but not before he had demonstrated it to me: "There are over 21,000 Post Offices in the UK, none of them connected by computer, nothing immediately checkable". He wanted a Roberts radio, I wanted money and oblivion, so we worked it to our mutual benefit. A visiting friend recognized the benefit of being involved in this venture and assisted by obtaining the necessary savings book, cow gum, and Stanley's white line chalk. These items were to find their way into the jail through a double-bottomed foil takeaway container of rice and peas. The glue and chalk in a hollow pen and a chewy mint sweet packet.

At this time, Diane ran off to Holland with a Liverpudlian distraction thief who had a widow's peak and thick glasses. The highpoint of his criminal career was the theft of several thousand pounds from a seaside undertaker. He also ripped off the band UB40 for a grand's worth of coke. I was devastated at the time, wrapping myself in a cloak of self-pity, thinking of the fitted carpets and the Hotpoint Ice Diamond fridge I had lavished on her. Not to mention the cookbooks I had sent home from Spain with all the high denomination pesetas in between the pages.

I ripped up a two-page letter that her new boyfriend sent me, basically saying no hard feelings and "we don't sit around talking about you". Somehow, a gold-coloured Sweep hand puppet with a black stitched nose and amber glass eyes had come into my possession while on the remand wing of the prison. My friend Mark, who shot a car dealer five times in a crime of passion, also had a puppet. I can't begin to imagine where these puppets came from, but I put the ripped-up letter inside mine and threw it in the landing dustbin as if concocting an ingenuous voodoo curse. Mark was disappointed that his puppet's pal had now gone.

This new boyfriend was to eventually OD and die in Brixton on the run from Ford Open Prison circa 1991. I remember one summer afternoon in Torquay when we were all friends and hard drugs hadn't yet got a real grip on us. We were watching a cricket match in Cockington meadows and the future myopic lover turned towards me pointing at his thin, midnight blue leather shirt, "I nicked this out of the same shop Ozzy Osbourne gets his clobber". Wearing a leather shirt in summer – honestly. I think they were eventually repatriated from Holland.

THE STUFF OF NIGHTMARES

POST INDIA, I made a diabolical Amsterdam trip with an accomplice in a light blue 345 Volvo. We stayed in the Hotel Continental, the Sex Museum on the corner over the road. The Continental was a favourite with ne'er do wells because they didn't ask for your passport straight away. Of course, getting some gear was the first thing I did when I arrived. I argued with a guy on a bridge who tried to swap bags on me. *Young and having the luxury of a death wish.* I would have quietly hummed 'Johnny & Mary' by Robert Palmer to myself, as I rapidly walked off with the smack in my clammy hand. I found a solace in this tune, it was my default when stressed. This was when the silver foil wrapped around Kit Kat chocolate bars was thick enough to smoke smack off. Scoring the speed from *The Other Place,* a bar run by Hell's Angels. They had a sign on the door with words to the effect: *Junkies will be killed.*

Driving back, my accomplice gives me two large packages which I put down my pants and leave the ferry as a foot passenger. I was so paranoid I felt like jumping from the ship into the harbour. Instead, I ran off into the container area and as a result I was collared. I'd been doing so much speed, drinking brandy, and the smack was long gone. It was the stuff of nightmares. I got dragged over to Customs and fuck knows how but I managed to dump one of the bags near some crash barriers and somehow shuffle the other one through customs. I'm sure they thought I was nuts and that's how I got through. I still had a packet of speed in my jacket top pocket.

Outside, I met the accomplice and produced the one bag which contained Mannitol, an Italian baby laxative. The other bag was the speed wrapped with a thousand blotters of acid, which was never part of the arrangement. I did wonder later if the acid had somehow leached. He went mental but I managed to convince him I could get back into the area where I dropped the drugs. Thankfully, he was stupid and even in this state I was convincing – and desperate. Needless to say, I never did go back. I hoover up the speed from my top pocket in a toilet. I was fucking freezing wearing a Duran Duran silk and cotton jacket. Coming back from Spain some months previously, I'd liked the look of a dressed mannequin in a boutique and bought the *tout ensemble*. In this summer attire I hitch-hiked up the windy hill out of Dover and somehow got back to Torquay. I later found out this guy was planning to rip me off for the run, not a lot of money of course – poetic. He was also instrumental in providing the Regional Crime Squad with information that later damned us.

I had a dream recently, it was after I'd read Oliver Sacks' book Gratitude, *a gift from my friend Harry. I was sitting on the floor with the accomplice from the Dover debacle. We're in an old-fashioned front room: mantelpiece, fireplace, three-piece suite, and flying ducks up the wall. There are toy cars on the carpet and we're pushing them around, but we are adults. We are all friends – there is no anxiety, only contentment. It might not sound a big deal, but I've carried a dreadful resentment for years and it has now left me. He died several years ago, drinking himself to death in a bedsit in Torquay.*

THE TEDDY BEAR HEAD

I ARRIVED IN Mumbai on an old 707 from Delhi at 10.30am and had to wait until the 11.30pm flight to Brussels – withdrawing plus Delhi Belly. Waiting, waiting to get a chitty for *Campa Cola*. Suffering the bureaucratic process – a legacy of Empire –before I got my drink. I had to keep myself together. The gear was sewn into the briefcase and I couldn't get at it. Miss Shepherd, an ambulance driver in Plymouth during World War II, had lodged with us when I was a child and taught me how to sew – and I'd made a good job of it. I remember my brother had a ginger teddy bear with a head that rotated. The head had fallen off and Miss Shepherd sewed it back on the wrong way around. I bet she had witnessed some terrible sights during the war.

The desperation down by the station in the Paharganj: I'd been told to stay out of the Paharganj, where the European junkies had sold their passports, where they'd try to hustle you, where they weren't getting out alive. I'd seen all this as I bought the matching cotton for the seams of the briefcase and the candle to strengthen the thread. I knew the score and couldn't help but reference *Midnight Express*: "Walk to the right, the left is communism". Stay cool and look mean – the smack is *our little secret*. Dressed like a man at C&A, I went in a scooter rickshaw to an antiques fair at Ashok Hotel in the diplomatic enclave of New

Delhi. Walked around the eternal flame at the Gandhi museum and took photos of traffic signs warning: 'speed thrills but also kills'. The Radial Roads off Connaught Place designed by Edwin Lutyens; roads big enough for cannon to fire down and too big for barricades but Haussmann had done it earlier in Paris. India Gate like Washington Square years later on my way to Brooklyn. The fan threatening to lift the hotel ceiling off and the humidity never relenting. Always tipping the room attendants, refilling the carafe way before bottled water. The fine tissue paper between freshly laundered shirts, the blood spots washed out of the sleeves. Up on the roof of the hotel, across the road from the Tourist Camp, I'd watch the birds in flocks circling.

On the way out, I killed time drinking disgusting Indian whisky in the vast departure lounge and speed walking to the European toilet – bunching toilet paper in my pants. *God will punish you for this Gerry, you can't get away with shit like this, and you're an utter cunt.* Worried about my own skin – God has nothing to do with this. Later, when I went towards the boarding gate for the Brussels flight there was a man wearing a Lungi kneeling down cleaning in one of the corridors, sweeping with a brush made from a tin can wrapped around some twigs. I gave him all the Indian money I had left, trying to assuage my guilt and hoping for a blessing.

Sabena Belgian World Airlines. It was the same hostess who I'd struck up a conversation with on the way over because she was marrying an Englishman. She administered me paracetamol and didn't put the corresponding number of pins in the headrest that count the quarter bottles of wine I was drinking. She gave me a break. White pins for white wine, red pins for red wine. Later, on the ground refuelling in the UAE while the cleaning crew scurried around the plane, I felt like death warmed up. Apparently, the contents of my briefcase could be the death penalty here.

Early morning, I arrived in Brussels – my baggage was labelled for Barajas Airport, Madrid. I slinked off into the airport to kill another four hours or so, looking for more alcohol. I noticed a sign to a chapel and then thought it would be a bit of a liberty popping in there for foxhole prayers. I met two oil workers from Gloucester, their address was on the heavy wooden cases they were lugging. They told me about installing equipment on oil rigs off Mumbai, saying the Indians wouldn't pay the extra to learn how to use the machinery.

SOOTHING SYRUPY CARLSBERG SPECIAL BREW

VISITS WERE CONDUCTED in an old prefabricated type of Nissan hut with a ribbed asbestos roof on which all manner of detritus was chucked from the cell blocks above. WRVS volunteers ran the canteen; tea, coffee, biscuits and sweet snacks were available. There were plain finger biscuits you dipped in chocolate and raisin Clubs, Marlboro reds and silver foil ashtrays. It was so depressing, everyone smoking and the grubby canvas-slung McLaren baby buggies rocking back and forwards to soothe their occupants. Visits from the girlfriend were about drinking Carlsberg Special Brew, smoking, and taking as many Valium as humanly possible to stay wrecked for a couple of days, while hoping to smuggle in a bit of contraband.

On one particular visit, Diane brought along a pal of mine, Martin, who I'd known for years. He resembled Neil Bell, the actor who played the part of Soz in the Shane Meadows film *Dead Man's Shoes*. Martin was dogged by bad luck. He had worked for Centrax, an engineering company near Newton Abbot. One day he lost his glasses case containing smack and works; a helpful fellow employee handed the case into management, who then called the police. He got a short prison sentence for that. Martin was an ex-grammar school boy and only child; his parents had once owned a bed and breakfast on one of the main approach roads to Torquay.

His father drove a Rover 2000 TC.

Martin's previous adventures involved robbing a chemist located in a row of traditional shops – the baker, the butcher, a newsagent, and the obligatory fish and chip shop, plus an area housing office. A Chinese takeaway would have been considered exotic then – this was part of a 1930s-built council estate during the mid-1970s in Torquay. He broke in on a Sunday morning when the pharmacist and his family were at church. He stashed some of the drugs in some local woods, never to find them again. Running off to Amsterdam, he got a job as a cook on a ship and plundered drugs from the sick bay. He'd previously stolen morphine ampoules from the lifeboats at Brixham but thoughtfully phoned the police straight away so they could replace them. While abroad, I think it was Turkey, Martin dosed up a rich American – all very Charles 'The Serpent' Sobhraj – stealing his money. Somehow Martin ended up in hospital; I don't think that was part of the plan. He managed to stash the stolen cash but, when it came time to leave the hospital, he couldn't locate it – every floor was identical. While playing the *preux chevalier* and trying to break up a fight on a Paignton council estate he lost an eye to a car aerial.

Correspondingly, there was a Scot I knew whose *modus operandi* was to give barbiturates to selected unsuspecting party-goers at his flat and then steal from them when they passed out. He too was to lose an eye in a fight. Weirdly, this experience led him to relocate to London, buy an acceptable Jaguar, and become an airport pick-up driver. He was called Bob – his long-term girlfriend left him at some point, and he eventually hanged himself. However, Scots Bob, along with Gypsy Tony, had once driven a Mini to Morocco and back to the Isle of Wight Festival with slabs of cannabis resin in the doors. They were to be ripped off by bikers at the festival. I was to hear the story individually from both of them years apart. Flying by the seat of their pants... the flimsy door cards on Minis with the cord you pulled down to open the door. It would have taken some balls to make that journey then, a round trip of approximately 3,500 miles: the border guards looking down at you in your small car, driving on primitive roads, low to the ground and nearer to the dogs. No credit cards then and a long way from home – no one to hear you scream...

Some years later, I visited Martin in the chaos of his mother's bungalow – it had a really treacherous entrance to and from the main road. The family bed and breakfast was long gone, and his father had died several years previously. Martin was now her main carer and she was in the throes of Alzheimer's. While we were talking, he took out his glass eye and popped it in his mouth to clean it. Martin was a gentle guy and I recollect him once showing me a picture of the actor Isabella Adjani he had painted while in jail, naïve but a reasonable likeness. Drugs and jail – in those days you never declared you were an addict, you got on with it with no methadone and no drug programme. If you said you had a drug problem, it would compromise any chance of an open prison where drugs were easier to get in. The horror stories of now, guys in jail owing drug dealers money and their families outside being threatened. In those days, to have drugs now and again was a treat, if it wasn't there you couldn't have it...

Martin was to be stabbed to death by a drunk in a Torquay council flat. It appears council estates had brought him nothing but bad luck. Martin could be irritating – harmless, but irritating in a repetitive sort of way; however, he certainly did not deserve to die for it. His retrieval skills were somewhat lacking. Many years later at Martin's funeral, I met Diane – we were older and so were the memories.

Martin was registered on Methadone, which was fortunate as it meant he was able to bring some in for me on a visit with Diane. Martin happened to mention that he'd seen the Liverpudlian distraction thief at a mutual friend's flat. I looked at Diane across the table and she looked away. Martin then realized what he'd let slip. I knew it was over. Desperate hand holding, probably on my part; but she just wanted to get the fuck out of the visiting room. I knew this was the breakup and it was going to be horrible and I was facing serious jail time for being an utter twat and was going to have to deal with it. This was the last visit I got from her. Two years later, I received a greetings card from her on my birthday, depicting a Helen Allington painting of a cottage. It had a London postmark.

A HERNIA, HIV AND CHERNOBYL

VALLI WAS A Brazilian I got to know. I'd see him around the jail, in the library mostly, sometimes on the exercise yard. He'd been busted at Heathrow with cocaine strapped to his body. Sheer bad luck. Valli had flown in from Charles De Gaulle, Paris, with a friend, maybe a mule. People tell you what they want you to know. Valli's story was how a trainee customs officer had patted his 'friend' down and everything was fine. Then, the customs guy officiating the training commented that he hadn't done it properly and then turned his attention to Valli asking, "You don't mind?" Not a lot Valli could say. He was busted.

Then there was Yogi, the ex-Heathrow baggage handler, and his tales of the Asian contingent. Days of hot-bedding (where the day shift sleep in the bed of the night shift worker) in mill towns up north, his early experiences of making money in the UK. Poor boys, a long way from home, some tempted to run the powder into the UK, nothing sophisticated, sheer numbers and fingers crossed. Yogi told me about one of his runners who was caught by British customs. Fresh-eyed (or as fresh-eyed as one could be after a long-haul flight), he had never been out of his village. The nylon shirt and plastic shoes, the beautiful blue-black sheen of the well-combed hair.

"Please could you come this way, sir?"

The boy is nervously sitting at the table, paperwork is perused, his passport examined – nothing is said. It's summer, the customs guy gets up and as he reaches for the air conditioning control, the young Asian screams, "Please, no, I tell you everything!" – thinking he was about to be tortured. Yogi thought this was hilarious.

Peter of the Luo tribe – tall, broad, and graceful, out of Kisumu, Kenya. Kilos of African bush through to Brixton, he was an old hand, good company, tremendous sense of humour, and very proud. He told me, "Gerry, I am always polite, but... Once they open the case, what is the point?" Several years later, I was to run some of his merchandise from Amsterdam through Heathrow – stinking, stalky bush. Peter told me he aspired to have multiple wives and to eat a kilo of the best beef a day. I never knew if he was teasing me.

At this time, the Thatcher government was shouting up the odds over the evils of drugs and, on the other side of the pond, Ronald Regan's wife – once a fabulous fellator to the stars – was telling everyone to 'Just Say No'. Of course, it wasn't working. Most of these guys were just trying to make a few quid and look after their families; there was nothing evil about them. I also met Northern British trawler men who'd brought in tons of cannabis and, of course, this was their first unsuccessful run – yeah, of course, jolly bad luck. It was a very democratic system in a prison, excluding Schedule 1 sex offenders. I learnt more from jails than I ever did from any diversity training in polite society.

Valli intrigued me; there was something sophisticated but, at the same time, dark about him. He vanished for a while. People ghosted out with no explanation. One day you noticed they just weren't there anymore.

I'd had a hernia for a while. I was going to get it put right privately after India but it never happened. Everything was later, I'll do it later. After I'd been sentenced, I tried to get it repaired as I wanted to go to the gym, but then found out the prison doctor had put the blocks on it. I made an appointment with him to question his decision. The Medical Officer present at this meeting let me tear into him. After a good vent, he said, "I think that's enough, King". This was my first encounter with Medical Officer Reed. I had a favourable opinion of him after this even though he was reputed to be an utter bastard. It was rumoured that his own son had stabbed him.

There is a melody to madness, a musicality to destruction. Everything has a rhythm: the initial tinkle of the small items and personal effects, before the big stuff starts. The bed, chair, bench table, being ripped off the wall, and if it got really bad, you'd hear the bed smashing against the stainless-steel toilet bowl and sink. The raised voices, the keys, the chains jangling, the scream of the rush into the room, the blunt thunking of bodies. The shouts recede with the anxiety, as do the clanging doors. The pack moves off. A call and response, a laugh, and an affirmation dressed up with expletive. I've heard it all before, but I don't want to hear it anymore.

As the old man said to me, "Once they close that door on you – you've lost".

When the landing officer told me on a Friday afternoon that I hadn't been granted parole, I replied, "Well, at least it's cornflakes tomorrow". We both laughed. I joined the Vegan Society; the dues were £6 yearly and they were based in Oxford on George Street near the bus station. There were benefits to this, including supplements to the usual menu, such as nuts, soya milk and, I think, yeast extract. I would swap tobacco for vitamin pills and cheat with a bowl of pilchards in tomato sauce every Sunday. I was concerned about a possible B12 deficiency. There was an exercise yard outside the Central Exchange Stores where clean clothes were collected on a weekly basis. A friend and I were walking around this yard a couple of days after the Chernobyl nuclear reactor meltdown had occurred and we were discussing the radiation fallout. He mentioned cattle more specifically sheep being affected by this disaster. I told him I was vegan (apart from the pilchards in tomato sauce). I'm sure he became a vegetarian.

I managed to get a date for the hernia operation. I think I had about a year left. Officer Reed said he wanted a word with me. He explained there are two men in the hospital wing, in fact they have the whole ward to themselves. Both are HIV positive. Reed asks me if I am prepared to associate with them, watch television and have meals together, when I return from the outside hospital. In order to make my decision I asked if I could read the guidance the Home Office has given him. Surprisingly he agreed. I didn't want fear to cloud the reality. I wasn't going to have sex or shoot drugs with either of them and certainly wouldn't be experiencing a North Vietnamese moment of direct blood transfusion as carried out in underground field hospitals in the Vietnamese Tunnels of Cu Chi.

I was taken to a hospital in Exeter and a prison officer was placed outside my room during my stay. My dad visited me along with my brother. I remember the book I took in with me was F. Scott Fitzgerald's *The Great Gatsby*. A tall, thin, male nurse with his Royal College of Nursing brooch tight to his throat asked if I wanted to shave myself or would I like him to do it. I did it myself in the shower. He kindly went out of his way and sorted out a B12 shot for me.

I recouped in the prison hospital wing and got to know Mark and his pal. They'd caught HIV in Oxford – a jail that doesn't exist anymore, it now being a high-end hotel. Mark told me the works were clean; he didn't see it coming. For such a bastard, Officer Reed had a lot of time for these two guys and he was decent to me. He'd arranged a greenhouse for them so they could grow tomatoes. He had compassion and a sense of humour – it was as if he functioned best under extreme conditions and these were extreme times. People didn't want to be anywhere near anyone with HIV. One night, in the television room, Mark sparked up a joint, took a few drags, and passed it to me. I knew Mark was watching me out of the corner of his eye. This was a moment of following the science - *you're not going to catch HIV from a teacup.* I think this was before Lady Di was hugging. I took the joint and a few pulls. No one searched these guys on visits or in the hospital wing, so it followed we were well-supplied with puff.

It turned out Valli had developed full-blown AIDS and was repatriated back to Brazil.

OXFORD TO LONDON VIA THE FLATLANDS COURTESY OF MASTERCARD

EVENTUALLY, IT WAS my release date and I was out back in the game again. Paul C. gave me a roll of tenners and a taste. I was living with an old flame, who had a penchant for Pop Tarts. This time around I was bleaching my works with a 10:1 bleach solution, sometimes taking the numbers off and putting butter on the rubber plungers. I attended an open day at Dartington College of Arts. I locked myself in the disabled toilet, did some gear, got thoroughly wrecked, and realized I was lost. 10 years later, I would find myself enrolling.

Torquay is a hiding to nothing, so I move to Oxford and get back with Diane. We rented a cottage at Yarnton from a pub landlord who had no right to rent it to us in the first place, but I only found that out after he disappeared to Spain. I work the nightshift at Oxford Exhausts on Woodstock Road while Diane does a bit of temping. I would go up to London directly after a 12-hour shift to score from a woman who always said, "I can get," on the phone. I was driving down Cable Street in a hired Volkswagen Polo with 1400 miles on the clock when the news came on the radio that Peter Tosh had been murdered in Jamaica. *You gotta walk, don't look back.*

I'm working at Oxford Exhausts the night Michael Fish got the weather forecast wrong, the storm of October 1987. The factory roof was rising and falling while we kept working, the steel presses hissing and stamping. Viscount Linley, Princess Margaret's boy, got first dibs on the exotic woods blown down in Kew gardens for his furniture and the Tantalus' with built-in compasses. On one London visit, we had our photos taken in a booth at Kings Cross. It was on the day of the devastating fire. We'd shop in Sainsbury's, drinking cans of wine, paying for the empties at the checkout, listening on a Sony Walkman to Talking Heads' *Little Creatures,* our headphones connected through a shared jack plug. Back to London, driving around trying to score with a friend, Pat. I smashed a tobacco tin lid down on the gear stick of her Renault 20, shaping a bowl to cook up in. I had to take rainwater from a dustbin lid because the radiator had anti-freeze in it. Getting a hit in the wrist at a well-lit crossroads on our way to Silvertown.

The work gets less as the excuses extend to every area of holding it together. We collect various I.D. along the way for the day when we'll have to run, credit cards with difficult signatures; gifts from the boosters who rob the bags from motors at the cash and carry. From a squat in E17, scoring, using, and scheming, then back to Oxford. We hire a car from a dealer out at Headington near the fibreglass roof shark and move on to Glastonbury. *And the beat goes on…*

The Somerset flatlands: long straight roads with drainage ditches either side, flood plains where snide new-builds pop up on concrete platforms to facilitate floating in the event of a Noah moment. I was looking for work, driving to a sub-contractor's bungalow in the middle of nowhere. A few shotgun pellet-peppered road signs were in evidence; it was like driving through a Bob Dylan ballad without the scale and with constant rain. I travelled these roads in all sorts of states, the most challenging being with Robbie, a lunatic acquaintance who I supplied with amphetamine from Bristol on a regular basis. Robbie enjoyed pulling the steering wheel, screaming, bawling and laughing, usually after we'd left cider farms buying and sampling the rough. The stinking effluvia of sheepskin factories on the outskirts of Glastonbury would clag the ditches. I'd have a film canister of speed and mix Pils lager with rough cider, listening to The Pretenders and The Clash on my Walkman, attempting to dream up an alternative to my low cal reality. I eventually got work as a carpenter's mate on the Yeovil ski centre, with my old pal John from Torquay.

I have an artist friend, a sculptor, who drove a black MG Magnet. We met in unconventional circumstances – he was doing time for importing dope for his own use. When he was busted, the drug squad officer kept using the phrase, "At the end of the day..." My friend took it to mean he'd be sent home at the end of the day – for him it was twenty-one months later. In many ways, he inspired me to pursue my writing; he represented another way to live, something for me to aspire to. His background was Happy Valley, Kenya – coffee had paid for him to go to Marlborough. During the 1980s, I would drive to his cottage near Dartmoor, sometimes turning up in taxis at diabolical hours, and stay with him for a couple of days trying to get off the gear. I would sit in the little orchard garden shivering with a poncho round me – his old cotton bed sheets ripping as I rolled over in bed sweating. Inevitably, I'd then tear back to civilization in a variety of ropey motors to score and score and score.

NICO AND THE HEARSE ON THE WAY OUT

"WHAT THE FUCK'S it got to do with yous?" barked my pal Billy in an aggressive manner to a short overweight security guard who had parked his van across the back of our motor. This was the beginning of the end days, the days that marked the time to the point where I'd had enough and couldn't keep doing this shit. We could hear the guard's dog moving about inside his fluorescently stickered white van and I was holding Nico on her lead. Nico is my black and brindle pedigree German shepherd bitch, with extremely fine markings and a friendly yet loyal demeanour.

Another Scotsman, Dalshey, who looked a bit like Ian McShane, rubbed his brow and just looked at Billy as if to say, *Shut the fuck up.* In the back of our motor was all manner of contraband: bottles of spirits and works with soot-blackened cooking spoons. We had no tax, no insurance, and probably no MOT... And not one driving licence between us. 'Listen to the Lion' by Van Morrison was a track I remember playing on the cassette. Sometime later, I found *Trainspotting* relatable as we'd done it in Devon with a mixed cast.

Earlier that morning I'd changed the back near-side tyre, which I'd noticed was flat when I'd come out to get my stash. I cut my hand on the exposed steel belt and had driven most of the night like that. The car was a black Ford Escort estate that somebody remarked looked like a hearse and the name had stuck. *Look after your equipment – always check the oil and water.* A general rule with older motors is to keep the petrol off the red so that the fuel pump doesn't suck the shit from the bottom of the tank. Another day, another dollar. I was on my own much of the time, no long-term relationship and even my dog Nico will soon be gone. The day before, we'd sold the part contents of an off-licence to the landlady of a roughhouse pub on a council estate in Torquay. Her boyfriend was a biker, much younger than her, and he helped us trundle the boxes up the side of a video shop and down the lane at the back of the pub. Cash changed hands and we were on our way.

The security guard probably wished he hadn't got involved. He pointed out we're on private property. I apologised and explained we were a gang of plasterers on our way to a job, adding that the dog needed some exercise and my pal was a bit short tempered as his missus had just left him. I threw in a bit of eye-rolling. Fortunately, everyone retained their pride and we moved on. Billy did this sort of shit and could have given Mark E. Smith lessons in chaos.

ALLEGRO VANDEN PLAS, 120 BASS ACCORDION AND MR. HANDOVER

THE PHOENIX ARTS Centre, Gandy Street, Exeter. I left the motor, an Allegro Vanden Plas, overnight in their car park. I was there for a poetry workshop; aspiring to be something other than the way I was living. I read the Mersey Poets and Johnny Clarke's *Ten Years in an Open Neck Shirt*, had a few copies of Ambit, and channelled John Betjeman whenever travelling on trains. I had literary pretensions but no real patience, no real technical inquiry; just knocking out a series of rhyming couplet rants. Sometimes, I'd be at the auctions on Okehampton Street, but I'd always touch base with the Arts Centre when in Exeter; it seemed to possess the mood of what I wanted to be.

I'd previously attended poetry evenings at Balliol College when I lived in Oxford a few years previously and read some of my work. I was labelled by some of the other participants as 'our ranter'. There was a pub, The Jericho Tavern, where some episodes of *Inspector Morse* had been filmed and many up-and-coming bands had played there. I'd met a guy through Balliol – his girlfriend was a photographer, something to do with the National Portrait Gallery – and he mentioned he could get me a spot reading between the bands; but, of course, I was too busy being a waster to get involved, going up to London and scoring dubious morphine from associates such as Bob the Booster, who used Acrow props to break through the walls of chemist shops. This particular morphine, when you shot it up, caused whatever limb you used to blow up like a balloon and itch so much that you would scratch to the point of bleeding. One night after I'd returned from London on the Oxford Tube coach, I went around to see a pal who lived in a caravan in a builder's yard – he was the security. He knew I was coming and there was a queue of half a dozen guys outside the caravan. When we all clambered inside it was like a subdued Father Ted dancing priest moment, but nobody was singing. I explained the side effects of the morphine; it didn't stop anyone using it. The sad thing about this situation was most of the punters were local rehab ex-residents.

Over a decade previously, I had been in a flat with about half a dozen other users. Jimmy and I had gone there to score, but there was no gear. We had a bottle of Tuinal barbiturates with us – not our drug of choice, but everyone in the place ending up using them. I remember one guy had just come out of jail for supplying smack to the great, great grandson of Charles Darwin. It's the nature of addiction – anything is better than nothing. Later that night, we found ourselves playing darts in a local pub that always stank of cats' piss, toeing the line on the oche with members of Torquay drug squad. This was the same pub Donovan, *Sunshine Superman*, would have frequented in the 1960s when he briefly lived in Torquay.

There were other associations with the Phoenix Arts Centre; creative and criminal. My last ever appearance at Exeter Crown Court and being asked to leave the dock as there was no evidence to offer against me. My two co-accused; one was to commit suicide after serving a life sentence for murder and the other – in addition to having teeth smashed out with a hammer for drug debts – was to be found dead of an overdose in a public toilet cubicle some years later, having to be identified by his fingerprints. (While he was dying, I was driving back from a book reading at Pallant House gallery in 2010). Correspondingly, as my associates dug in deeper, I was more determined to get away from this existence, everything was a yet. This was a tiresome story of a petty and demeaning episode involving collectable stamps swathed in inferior paper that fingerprints couldn't be lifted from. I left the court with a solicitor's clerk, ex-Flying Squad, who drove a Mercedes Benz. I treated him to lunch at the Arts Centre, probably veggie – an anti-climactic celebration. He saw the result understandably as a victory. I wished my life wasn't as sordid as it was, and my friends were cooler. In the course of conversation, he asked if there were any valuable items left at the address the stamps came from. My friend Ali the Turk had said to me one night, "You gotta stop this, you'll go to prison in and out – your nose will be broken, you'll lose your looks". That is a speech that, weirdly, I never forgot; so basic, yet so profound, and this coming from a man standing outside a property he had once gambled away. I never considered I had 'looks' but it was certainly that loss of youth, the getting older in a blue-striped shirt. Vanity or maybe the prospect of either maturity or death, and profound statements are never made at the breakfast table.

On this occasion, I'd booked into a bed and breakfast near the Arts Centre and I remember coming down to breakfast with a bottle of wine and the local Torquay newspaper. There was a story in the paper about a girl who I went to school with. It was the same girl who was crying in the newsagents when Jimi Hendrix died. The story was about her disabled brother and how she was trying to raise the money to take him for a cruise on *Queen Elizabeth 2*.

While I was in Exeter, I managed to sell a Hohner 120 Bass accordion for £140 to a music shop on the high street. They paid by cheque and while cash was preferable, I understood this was a good price and I'd have to find a way round it. I noticed on the cheque that the main bank branch was in Teignmouth. Taking the coast road back to Torquay I located the bank – near a jewellery store I'd once sold forty pounds' worth of Churchill crowns – and explained the situation to a teller who brought the manager over; a Mr. Handover. I went into my spiel supporting my story with published poems and a letter from the artist Peter Howson, explaining I'd had an opportunity to read at the Edinburgh Fringe Festival and I intended to meet Peter Howson in Glasgow to discuss the possibility of a collaboration. Opportunity was knocking but time was against me and I needed to get to Scotland. Some months previously, I'd seen Howson's work in the *Sunday Correspondent* newspaper and contacted his gallery enclosing a few of my poems. He'd replied favourably suggesting we could do something with his paintings and my writing. I also showed Mr. Handover a copy of the Bristol magazine *Rampage* in which some of my work was published. Further adding that while I still played piano, I didn't feel the same passion for the accordion therefore I'd reluctantly sold it.

Fourteen £10 notes were trousered with a handshake and an aside – "Don't spend it all on beer". Mr. Handover was a decent guy who had given me the benefit of the doubt. Admittedly I couldn't play the piano and never heard from Peter Howson again, although

I did keep writing – I believe he had a nervous breakdown after being the official war artist for the Bosnian conflict and found God.

When I arrived back in Torquay, I went around to the Jimi Hendrix crying girl and gave her some money toward her brother's cruise. Reminding me of the cleaner at Bombay airport and me trying to assuage my guilt – I would've made a competent catholic.

DISTRACTION NUMBER EIGHT

With this new Coronavirus everything is so uncertain, and my nearby Spanish neighbours love a party, the Scandinavian finance interns on my landing are partial to a Friday night blow-out as well. The reality is I'm living in a low-rise tenement block with a number of other people in a reasonably concentrated area. Upstairs, Noaim – when he isn't studying – is a Deliveroo rider, and told me he was getting busier. Covid-19 coming out of a wet market in Wuhan, China. Haven't we been here before, at least in a fictional sense and, let's face it, isn't it getting harder to differentiate between the realistic and fictional senses? During the 1970s, there was a television series called Survivors, it related the experience of a group of people, in the UK, who had survived an apocalyptic plague pandemic. The virus had been accidentally released by a Chinese scientist and had then run riot across the world. The survivors move from location to location, usually farmhouses with muted acoustics, banging doors, and beige Aga cookers. Most dialogue is of the best BBC received pronunciation variety, bar that coming from the occasional token yokel, and every so often a manhandled young woman will be saved by a brawny bearded man wearing tweed. Not forgetting the willowy brunette – cheesecloth is a feature – changing the bandages of the brawny bearded man, the scenes heavy with sexual tension and good teeth. Land Rovers, wax jackets, muddy tracks to homesteads, and abandoned quarries feature heavily, and of course they end up safely in the wilds of Wales.

I decide I'm going to Wales tomorrow – my pal Kabir on the top floor, a teacher, has a spare key to my flat and said he'd look after the plants. I have a rail ticket, but it is booked for the following month, as I always take my holiday in April.

If they start giving me a hard time at the station, this is what I'll say...

There was no need to say anything when I got to Paddington – the guards weren't even checking tickets, just asking what your destination was and directing you to your train. Everyone was getting a squeeze; it was as I imagined an evacuation to be. Why does it take a catastrophe before people are reasonably civil to each other? On my train, there were only three people in the quiet carriage all the way to Cardiff.

Entering into this government-sanctioned, pseudo semi-retirement and introduced to a new word: furloughed, being granted a paid leave of absence. I consider the ducking and diving, the self-employment, the paid guests, Airbnb, and poaching for cash nights. Now avoiding people in this context for the fear of contagion, becoming familiar with the new ritual of keeping your distance, keeping your mask on and washing your hands frequently. Searching for a precedent – Survivors aside – and landing back at a 1970s Portland Borstal: in a workshop, paint-spraying bed-ends destined for UAE prisons, wearing a mask and being given a pint of milk a day for this chore. What will we drink now? I'm sticking to coffee as nothing ever really made me forget... only in unconsciousness but, even then, the dreams got breached.

While I was waiting for my connection at Cardiff, I got talking to a guy who confirmed I was on the right platform for the Burry Port train. It turned out he was an ASLEF union representative. Everything felt like preparation – getting ready. It's hard to explain but I did feel like I was sneaking into Wales on the 18th March 2020. I arrived a month earlier than planned.

CRASH

MY BROTHER IAN came into quite a respectable amount of money through a compensation claim that had been rolling on for nearly a decade. Statistically, a scandalous percentage of people who are awaiting compensation pay-outs, especially where head injuries are involved, end up committing suicide. The insurance companies are not like governments seeking short-term election, these companies hone their skill over generations. They know how to work it and, whatever their field of expertise, it just gets stronger.

I often wondered what Ian did all day. It was almost as if his life had been on hold for 10 years, the claim all-consuming. The pain medication, the automatic black Ford Mondeo supplied by the government mobility scheme, and of course the thickening files of correspondence on first-name terms with clerks and solicitors, billing every hour like a girlfriend experience.

In the beginning, just after the accident, he didn't even have a phone, and I'm talking about a landline. This was during the last few days of October 1988. I remember because it was near my birthday. Of course, he wouldn't tell you how he eventually got a phone and certainly wouldn't accept the accident was partly his fault. The deal was that I would sort out a phone for him and pay for the installation, if he kept a suitcase in his flat overnight that I'd be bringing from London.

It was a cold, slow Monday evening when I flew into a subdued Heathrow from Schiphol, Amsterdam. I walked through the 'nothing to declare' channel. I was hanging on to the thought: *I'm skint and when you've got nothing, you've got nothing to lose.* The luggage carousel next to the one I collected my case from was the Israeli airline El Al and a couple of armed policemen were holding the chains of Alsatians. Stinking, stalky African bush. This was a worst-case scenario and the dice were rolling. The date was 9th January 1989, the day before a BMI flight had crashed onto a motorway at Kegworth, Leicestershire. I flew in on BMI.

Some months earlier, I'd been on a coach coming from London to Bristol. The coach stopped at Heathrow. I had a large sports bag with me, and in the bag was 10 kilos of badly-wrapped resin. At the airport, on the coach outside the terminal, I could smell the hash. Big deal.

This time I'm on the inside looking out. I make my approach wearing my faithful double-breasted grey Dior, shirt and tie, smart haircut, clean shoes and a Crombie overcoat draped round my shoulders, aspiring to the Robert Palmer look: 'Addicted to Love'. Swinging the suitcase onto the trolley, I tail-gate a backpacker as customs invariably stop them. Proffering my pristine European visitors' passport, they give it a cursory glance, my apparent quiet confidence serving me well. Clearing customs, I walked down to the Underground. I think I travelled to either Northfields or Boston Manor where a couple of pals were waiting in a Vauxhall Nova. I recall Talking Heads' 'Television Man' and Eric Clapton's 'Wonderful Tonight' being part of the soundtrack while necking duty-free Courvoisier as we hit the M4 journeying south to Devon, dropping the case off for the night with Ian.

Summer 1998, Cargiant, White City, London, near Kensal Green cemetery: I'm standing on a polished floor in a showroom of several series 300 and 400 Lexus cars, none of which are over three years old. Ian has a banker's draft for 15 grand. We'd looked at Mercedes and BMWs but came back to the Lexus. He asks me, "Which one shall I get?" I go up to the customer service desk and find out which cars have a full-service history. There was one, Kensington green with an ivory leather interior. It had been leased to a media company and the bottom line was just over 16,000. I was living very much on a budget at this time as I had recently started a three-year degree course at Dartington College of Arts.

Ian decides to buy it, we go into an office and the paperwork is sorted. The car salesman is also called King and comments, "Well, here we are – we three Kings". I force a blokey laugh, all the time thinking this is a diabolical waste of money. The motor deal includes a Club Lexus membership with all sorts of benefits attached like a glossy quarterly magazine with holiday, golf deals, and most importantly for me, a Tate membership.

Late November 1998, I flew back to Heathrow from Chicago and Ian picked me up in the Lexus. I'd bought him a silver money clasp from Cartier on Michigan Avenue – the Magnificent Mile. I still have a small leaf, now sellotaped to a page in a journal that blew in the door of the shop when I was making the purchase.

During the late 1990s, I'd catch the National Express from Torquay coach station to London, arriving at Victoria. The past would always make an appearance when I was in this vicinity, as I once knew someone called Steve who lived on Lupus Street, Pimlico. His wife, an Australian, worked as a hostess in the West End. It was a marriage of convenience involving a visa. The last time I'd seen him was around 1988 prior to the Amsterdam trip, on our way through. He'd given me a loaded works full of smack – I'd used it as we drove toward Heathrow. He was never to be trusted and it was certainly not a friendship that endured. I'd pass their long-vacated flat on my way to visit Tate Britain. It seemed like another lifetime. On arrival, I would make straight for the pre-Raphaelites in the 1840s gallery, Waterhouses' *Lady of Shalott* and, of course, the iconic *Ophelia* by Millais. I slowly developed confidence, feeling less of an outsider and comfortable enough to occasionally comment to a fellow visitor, but always hoping Brian Sewell wouldn't appear next to me and ask a question.

When Tate Modern opened in May 2000, I would enjoy the members lounge, generally wandering around and getting familiar with the building and making friends with *The Handsome Pork Butcher* by Francis Picabia and Roland Penrose's *Portrait*; old familiars in the Natalie Bell building on Level 2. I didn't know how to express why these works affected me in the way they did, and I remember someone saying to me, bizarrely enough at Dartington, "Art never saved anyone's life." I couldn't be bothered to challenge them, thinking not only of my own experience that I didn't like to share, but mostly of the Jewish émigrés fleeing Europe and teaching at Dartington in the late 1930s.

I moved to Bristol from Torquay. I remember the last time Ian and I were in London together we went to Tate Modern. Ian had driven from Devon in the Lexus to meet me and we caught the train up to London. I knew there was a distance between us. There was almost a correlation between not understanding some of the artwork, not getting it, to how our familial relationship was tuning out. Even though we were in the same space and shared many past experiences, there was a barrier only broken momentarily with smoking, drinking, and eating. I still smoked then. We would stand on the balcony looking over the Millennium Bridge to St Paul's Cathedral. It seemed unable to emit any spiritual redemption his way.

Ian kept that Lexus for years; the warranties and club benefits would have receded incrementally along with the value. In 2008, as I drove toward Dartmouth, I remember seeing it parked up near Oldway Mansion, Paignton in Devon. I continued to visit Tate without the membership, paying for the occasional exhibition. The works of art are still there, if not on display then in the collection. I take comfort in that thought. I often wonder about Ian, but life has taught me you cannot go back. I know I'll never see him again.

DISTRACTION NUMBER NINE

I don't know if it was stress. I'd considered at one point it was psychosomatic. Was it something I had eaten or maybe I wasn't exercising enough? I'm a great believer in making the effort, especially now in this time of uncertainty, in this time of Corona. "Wear the mask – don't wear the mask. Wear the mask like Ned Kelly". I remembered I'd had this complaint before and I find as I've got older ailments return, turning up like the Lynchian Log Lady, just standing staring, taunting me. I had been waking up most mornings with a really bad stomach ache. Still tired I would twist and turn, trying to hold on to dreams, the sounds of outside leaching inside. Eventually, I'd make myself get up and go downstairs to prematurely organize breakfast. I relish some self-discipline and a sense of order.

The 'Monarch of Mono', a DJ pal, texted me late on a Thursday afternoon,

Gerry call me please. Glenn is in hospital and is dying.

I rushed straight out to the garden, as if I needed air, pacing up and down, responding with misty eyes to the grim news. I find out that Glenn has aggressive liver cancer and only has weeks to live. Glenn is my friend; a performer, writer, poet, and teacher. It transpired his wife had arranged for him to be at home, to be comfortable in his final days. I kept hoping he'd rally round, that we'd be able to chat on the phone, but he didn't make it.

Several poetesses set up a WhatsApp group and we'd all keep in contact monitoring our ailing laureates' dire situation. I'd romanticize the grim reality, visualizing the Henry Wallis painting of Chatterton the boy poet dramatically draped across his bed – Glenn was 65. The cancer was ferocious, taking him down in just over a week, pneumonia kicking in, with Covid-19 the coup de grace. 6.00 a.m., Monday 4th May 2020. His obituary will be in The Guardian. I will be slightly jealous of this, projecting I probably won't get a mention. Later, his wife telephones and during our conversation she tells me that on one ward Glenn had been in there were two homeless guys, one who kept constantly farting and the other who listened to Country and Western music on the radio. We laughed knowing Glenn would have used that as material. I cried for him and I cried for myself. The last time we'd met there had been a falling out over the pruning of an apple tree in his garden. We'd had artistic differences before, like handbags at dawn, but always made up. However, this time somehow life had got in the way and no Christmas cards had been exchanged last year. I remember a girlfriend once saying to me you should always leave a house on good terms because that might be the last memory you have of someone.

I have a photograph of Glenn and myself pulling faces in front of a Gilbert and George poster in the gift shop at Tate Modern. We'd been referred to as Bristol's answer to Gilbert and George after taking part in a performance at Bath's Fringe Festival some years ago. When he came up to London we'd always go to Tate, it was a ritual we both loved. That's how I remember us, swanning about looking at art, but I also remember what he'd taught me. My love of Andy Warhol came from our friendship; I'd always liked Warhol and as I got older a deeper knowledge developed, encouraged by Glenn. He also taught me about performance and delivery. Sometimes he underestimated himself and I remember when he'd asked me to come along to a novel writing class he was teaching at the Arnolfini in Bristol, as he was concerned about lack of attendance. I went along to support him but found myself drawn in, realizing just how little I knew about what I'd taken for granted.

My stomach pain had been occurring since I arrived in Wales (self-isolating for two weeks) on Wednesday 18th March 2020 – nearly a week shy of the official lockdown. I made an appointment at the local surgery to see the doctor on the following Tuesday. Firstly, there was a telephone consultation to establish I didn't have a temperature or a persistent dry cough and then I was granted access to Doctor Sharma. It was all very anti-social in a professional clinical way – social distancing, dancing around each other, in one door and out the other. My stomach was prodded and I was told nothing serious was wrong, but for my own peace of mind I should have a blood test. I was given a card with a phone number, so I rang and made an appointment for Thursday morning.

I'm a Scorpio and apparently Scorpio's are prone to ailments around the stomach and groin area. I imagine in California or Totnes in Devon there are extensive and expensive courses dedicated to this planetary physical focus, allowing for self-obsession. Glenn had come along with me for support when I had to go for a colonoscopy procedure, this would have been about 2005 when I was still living in Bristol. While a CD player provided a disco soundtrack, an Australian nurse asked, once I was in position so to speak, if I wanted to watch the examination on a monitor. I declined.

The falling out over the pruning of the apple tree wasn't about the tree. The tree was blameless. In London, a few years previously, Glenn had left my flat after I made some remark about him not making enough effort regarding the selling of his book. Up to this point, we'd spent about three days together and through a contact I had negotiated his book *Still Searching for the Big City Beats* into the Staff Picks section of Foyles in Charing Cross Road. I felt he wasn't taking full advantage of this opportunity. What I did not appreciate was the fact Glenn was content at this point, he had got the book out there so to speak, and it was me projecting my own insecurities.

Before I slinked out into the night at 1:30 a.m. from his home in Bristol, the last word Glenn probably ever spoke to me was: "Goodnight". I drove to Wales. The M4 was closed in sections for maintenance causing me to detour through small winding village roads. I was getting tired and crazy thoughts relating to guilt and superstition were going through my head.

I watched the Jesse Eisenberg, Imogen Poots film Vivarium the other night. I'm sure Glenn would have appreciated the sinister low one-directional lighting and the Hopperesque application of green and orange, as well as the almost Warholian monosyllabic delivery by the actors. I remember when I'd go around to his flat in Montpelier, Bristol, before he was married. The meal would always be a microwave Tesco curry with small individual bowls of salad, consisting of cucumber, tomato, and sliced iceberg lettuce. We would eat on a Formica-topped drop-leaf 1960s table on the landing. If I ever stayed, sleeping on the big black Habitat leather sofa bed, I would always take the battery out of the clock in the front room. I remember one evening we watched, with a French friend of ours called Loic, a video of Johnny Cash singing 'Hurt' by Nine Inch Nails – we all had tears in our eyes by the end.

I'm in Llanelli for my blood test. It's raining and I'm standing under a crow-black umbrella in the car park of an industrial estate. There is a man in front of me – I find out later he is Mr. Thomas. We are socially distanced. Through a chain-linked fence, there is a patch of rough wasteland and I can see scrapped cars parked awkwardly.

I remember going to Bournemouth with my dad when I was a kid and visiting a family who operated one of the roundabout rides on the fairground. Their boy had an Austin pedal car with the flying 'A' on the bonnet that opened and a little tin-lidded boot with a chrome handle. This type of collectable pedal car could now be found displayed in the kitchen of a start-up entrepreneurs converted Cornish barn. There was something so comforting about riding that pedal car down the garden path, the tyres gently kissing the concrete lips of the poured sections. Flashes of those early memories out and about with my dad, driving around London and later Devon; he must have told me lots of things, and I wish I could remember them all now. Visiting friends and relatives, returning home late and my dad picking me up off the bench seat as a slow shushing car passes, lights licking our glass and the quiet night amplifying the gentle conversation between Mum and Dad, "All right, love, I'll get the door". Years later I'd explore the local council scrapyard where the smashed and twisted cars would wait to be crushed. I would clamber about in them, discovering under the carpets a section of spanking new sprayed metal, pristine as when it left the factory, or the electrical loom behind the dash with signed inspection stickers still bright. I was captivated by these finds and wanted it all to be new again.

My mum once told me about bodies carried out of a bombed

cinema in London during the war. There wasn't as much as a blemish on them, not a mark. I am old now and things are wearing out. There are some sections that still look reasonably okay, but I know I'm wearing out. I try to do gentle exercise every morning and go for long walks. In my fifties, I used to jump onto the bonnet of my car and my daughter would say, "Why are you doing that?"

I'd reply: "Because I can". I was standing by a stream the other day; there had been some serious rainfall, the water was running fast, and the stream was partially blocked. I considered pulling a few logs and branches out of the way and jumping across, but I hesitated.

Mr. Thomas and I are standing in the rain, socially distanced in the rutted car park, waiting for our names to be called. We start talking about the pandemic and how it had been handled, somehow this leads us to showing each other our respective union membership cards and I see his name on his Unison card. I leave him with my umbrella when I go in.

I sent Glenn a card and his last email to me read,

> This is a short one chum. Your words were goood. Thanks. I have developed Hepatitis C. It has gone so far there is no dodging it. No wonder I was always tired. It's all a bit much. I will write more. Later. Goodbye x

RUNNING ON EMPTY

NEVER STUCK AT a trade. My whole existence was futile and pathetic, I was under no illusion, all I wanted to do was feel better and I accepted this was a really selfish way to live. Occupation: Wanker – in a first world country full of opportunity. I held my hands up, waved the white flag; at a drug service in Exeter I signed up for a methadone script, the sheer amount of sugary shit ultimately doing a job on my teeth over four years. However, I'm not totally dissing speed's contribution in dental decay. When I eventually got into rehab, I was asked how long I'd been registered on the juice. I said three years – that's what it did, acted as a thief of time and dissolver of calcium. I tried to hold on to some semblance of normality prior to this; working two jobs a day to support my habit and not break the law. Grafting on a building site, I remember digging out a trench in a flooded basement as the water came over my boots and when I moved on from this job, the gaffer said they'd always be work for me if I wanted it... Always try and leave on a high note.

It seemed the glass got thicker, the alarms louder, and I was tired. It felt like everything was too late, that I'd never make up for lost time. I watched the blank shops zip past, my cheek on the motorcyclist's back, clutching a big canvas laundry bag between myself and the rider I had put my faith in. I had an apparition of massive Kenny Everett waving hands: *Praise the Lord. Do you believe? Yes I do! Just get me out of this shit, don't crash.* Weight distribution is important. I learnt that loading vans with booze in Calais, always stack up from the middle toward the front of the cab. We hit the comfort zone of the council estate, the sagging concrete post, chain-linked fences, and weaved effortlessly through the double-buggy-wide lanes.

Apparently, one definition of insanity is repeating the same things and expecting different results. Driving a borrowed car, Frank the cross-dressing burglar pulls up on the pavement outside the local Co-op. I then go through the front doors with a hammer. For whatever reason, I couldn't see the vodka and so I grabbed handfuls of whisky. I really didn't care. We'd been up speeding for a couple of nights and, of course, there was always the methadone playing like a backing track. I ended up crashing out on the settee in the house of a lunatic, but this only became evident when I woke up in hospital.

The clues should have been there. The guy was a bricklayer and going out with an ex of mine, he was probably one of the first Red Wall supporters. On his mantelpiece, pride of place was a photograph of him shaking hands with Margaret Thatcher circa 1986 when she'd visited the Riviera Centre, a project he was laying bricks at. It transpired he viciously attacked me in my sleep and I wasn't the first person he'd done this to. He was certainly one of the many that whisky didn't agree with. I was told at the hospital I was very lucky as the 'Max Factor' team were on that night, specialists who dealt with car crash face injuries. One of my eyes had been really badly cut. When I came around a policeman was sitting next to my bed. He asked me if I wanted to press charges against the guy who'd attacked me. I said no. I couldn't bring myself to go for a criminal injuries claim either. My pride was hurt and I always accepted that if I was outside the law I couldn't play both sides of the fence, so to speak. It took me a while to realize that some of my criminal contemporaries weren't sharp operators but merely informants when it suited them.

My top had been cut off when I'd been admitted and my torso was covered in bruises. I pulled my jeans on and, wearing a hospital pyjama top, discharged myself. I knew my face was a mess but I could function. My life played out like a drama in the street, I had to get from A to B and no one could do it for me. I realized the bastard had robbed me but, luckily, I found a crumpled note in the watch pocket of my jeans so I was able to get a taxi. I looked like shit: blood all over my jeans, my hair matted with blood, and stitches over one of my black eyes. I probably told the taxi driver I'd been in a car crash but he would have guessed there was more to this due to the route we took. First stop an off-licence for a quarter bottle of spirit, then the chemist for my script, and finally to my dealer for some gear. I'd been in similar situations before but it really hurt this time. Money would have afforded me privacy, delegation – a luxury I didn't have.

Once upon a time at a courthouse in North Devon, I was charged with robbing a chemist in a picturesque market town. I was standing in the court wearing a paper forensic suit looking like the main character in *Eraserhead*. I was certain if I couldn't talk to the magistrate I'd be remanded in custody. My black dress suit and leather-soled Italian dance shoes had been sent off to forensics – this was a *Blues Brothers* period, sans ex-Illinois police car and levitating nuns. The defence solicitor tried to deter me, and I told him if he didn't let me address the court I'd start shouting and be in contempt. I had nothing to lose – a familiar situation. I addressed the bench, "Your worships, I can understand your reluctance in granting me bail…"

At that point one of them piped up in a *Dad's Army*, Captain Mainwaring voice, "Who said we are reluctant?" We're cooking on gas! Dad stood surety and I went on digging a deeper hole after a stunning train journey on one of the most scenic routes in Devon between Barnstaple and Exeter St. Davids; I remember being lifted as the beauty touched me.

I recall Dad telling me when he realized he had to stop boxing. The punches began to hurt more and it was torturous making the weight and getting in shape. He was a journeyman fighter and he knew he had to stop. He'd watched some of his pals destroy themselves; they kept going, giving the young fighters their bodies to practice on, and they were royally fucked when the final bell rang.

I was alone now. I'd brought this on myself and I knew only I could extricate myself – a thought that I found terrifying. I did a lot of thinking, licking my wounds in my bedsit, with some music and my books. I made forays to the off-licence and chemist – late night wanderings and a few doctors' bags. Regan had been found dead a couple of months previously. He was diabetic and I think he forgot to take his insulin, perhaps on purpose. The last time I saw him he came to Ian's flat where I was staying while Ian was away in Spain. It would've been about 10 in the morning. He spilt a glass of booze on the carpet and fetched a cloth to mop it up, but he started to wipe clean an area unaffected by the spillage. I said to him, "Regan, I can't help you because I can't help myself". He left and almost immediately there was a knock at the door. It was my brother's landlord, who happened to be a Christian, asking for rent. By the time I managed to get outside to look for Regan, he had disappeared and that was the last time I saw him, just his coffin at the crematorium. Always the 23rd Psalm – I should have walked with him when he was still around.

It was four in the morning again and I was rereading one of my favourite books featuring stories by various American Beat writers; it had been a present from a prison teacher called Rosie Howells. The book lived in a brown, rattly glass-front bookcase. I was drinking Stonehouse filtered cider, smoking roll-ups, and killing time until the chemist opened to collect my prescription. I'd walk there and back hoping I wouldn't bump into anyone. I was full of shame and my confidence was utterly depleted. The realization hit me that even if someone turned up on my doorstep and gave me a bundle of money it would be no good to me. I was broken and the controls were damaged. Even during the worst winter dawn, looking into the kitchenette mirror with its crazed silvering under 40W bulb, I knew there was something better. Many years later, it got back to me that a close friend had remarked to a drug counsellor, "It was like Gerry had a get-out plan". But, I really didn't – more a blind faith.

Some months later, I finally made the commitment and went into a psychiatric facility to dry out first from the drink. They prescribed me Librium to stop the shakes but kept me on the juice until the rehab. I asked my pal Billy to bring in some films on VHS and he brought me *The Silence of the Lambs*. I went off to bed leaving the tape running for fellow residents in the recreation room. The next morning I was called into the office. Apparently, there was a pornographic film playing after the main feature. There would have been a speech about vulnerable disturbed people and how thoughtless I was. The last film Billy and I saw together was *Dirty Rotten Scoundrels*, starring Steve Martin and Michael Caine. It was a sunny day and we watched it in his front room with the curtains drawn. I would have later walked past the crematorium and the graveyards on both sides of the road, down a hill and up another one to the hospital.

Billy was to visit me a few times while I was in there. I remember us talking in the laundry room one evening and him saying, "I don't know how you can do this".

I replied, "I've got to". He then asked me for a couple of quid toward a bottle of cider. We later always kept in touch; I saw myself as leading by example, but he didn't make it. Billy overdosed having that last hit and was dumped in a garden the day before he was due to go into a treatment centre. If he'd lived, I know he'd have loved Bob Dylan's song 'Key West'.

DISTRACTION NUMBER 10

My phone is on vibrate. I see the WhatsApp message is from the Doc in Chicago.

> Bad news my son. Got a text a couple hours ago from Todd's roommate in Oregon telling me she found Todd dead in his room Friday evening. I talked to him midweek at length and he seemed fine. So I'm thinking it was natural causes. He was a wonderful guy and he loved my kids. As you can imagine, I'm kind of at a loss for words but I thought you needed to know.

I'm on a train travelling through South West Wales, towards Burry Port. It's still lockdown but I'm returning from an essential journey to London as my flat has flooded. I'm in the quiet carriage at a table seat reading a nonfiction book, *Nomadland: Surviving America in the Twenty-First Century.* The book is written by Jessica Bruder, an investigative reporter. I'm alone in the carriage reading of elderly Americans ruined by the 2008 financial crash, living in recreational vehicles and following minimum wage work around the States, echoing the dust bowl pain of the Great Depression. It's pouring with rain and the train is coming into Port Talbot, passing the steaming Tata steelworks with the landmark burn-off torch flaming. I see my reflection in the window as I look out toward the town where a Banksy had been stencilled on a corporation garage wall. I feel like ghosts surround me. This relentless rain reminds me of Berlin, coming out of the U-Bahn station on Brunnenstraße near the Ocelot bookshop. It rained so hard I felt like crying and wanted to go home. I was wearing a shower-proof, classic, Jaeger ivory Macintosh and thought of Michael Caine playing Harry Palmer in the film *Funeral in Berlin.* I trudged the streets to an Airbnb with a platform bed near Rosenthaler Platz. I noticed the brass cobbles with Jewish names.

The Doc is of Jewish ancestry. This fucking rain and the ghosts and now Todd has joined them. He had something of the Tim Robbins about him. I knocked about with Todd in Chicago during the fall of 1998. Rich, uniquely American memories flashback as I roll through South West Wales. There was a phone call from Todd – I answered it in the witch's hat of the Doc's house on Belmont and Hoyne opposite the Beat Kitchen. He knew I wanted to meet Chicago's famous son, the Pulitzer Prize winning writer and broadcaster Studs Terkel, and told me to get down to the Art Institute as Terkel was going to be there. Frederick Wiseman, the documentary filmmaker, was launching his latest project, *Public Housing*, and Terkel was going to be on the panel.

Terkel arrives in a cab and, as he gets out, I ask him if he is Studs Terkel. He waves his walking stick in the air and shouts, "I sure as hell hope I am". I had taken with me a copy of his hardback book *Working* that the Doc had given me. I also had a first edition paperback copy of Nelson Algren's *Chicago, City on the Make.* He signed both of them in the lift we shared. Generally, an author will never sign another writer's book, but Algren was a close friend of Terkel.

Another day in Lincoln Park, Chicago, Todd and I are at a film production company's headquarters. As we go into the building, there is a homeless guy pushing a shopping trolley with a fire burning in a brazier and Todd presses some bills into his hand. In the foyer is a large elaborate fountain. We are to drive to Racine, Wisconsin, to collect the first rushes of a film called *Spirit of Carnaúba*. I seem to remember Todd knew someone in the production office and that's how we happened to be doing this gig. The film was about the son of the founder of Johnson Wax retracing his father's 1935 flight to Brazil in the same amphibious Sikorsky S-38 plane. Carnaúba palm, whose wax is the toughest in the world, was the key ingredient in nearly every Johnson furniture wax product at that time. We collected the cans of 35mm film from a motel in Racine and dropped them off at a laboratory in downtown Chicago before midnight. We were driving around during this time in a black series 5 BMW. The deal was Todd had to drop off a Chicago-based businessman at O'Hare and collect him when he flew back from Miami. In the meantime, Todd could have use of the car. We stopped off at a shopping mall in Kenosha where I bought some clothes for my daughter Alexi from the Oshkosh outlet and tried some Nikes on reduced from $120 to $20 but realized I didn't need them.

In Burry Port later that evening, the Doc and I speak on the phone as I wander up the lane to the chapel. He tells me that Todd was adopted, and his birth mother was from Wales. We reminisce and the Doc tells me that he was going to come to the UK this summer with Todd before the Corona reared its ugly crown.

A few days later, the Doc texts me from a legendary 1950s burger bar in Milwaukee that I'd visited with him back in '98. He was there with his children Devon and Phoenix. Their mother – the Doc's ex-wife, the voluptuous Gigi – is a talented tattoo artist and sword swallower in New Orleans.

This weekend I had scrambled eggs with mushrooms and then mint chocolate chip ice cream at Kopp's. These were my first two meals on board the USS

United States when I came to America. It had an indoor and outdoors pool and a movie theatre where we saw Sinbad and the Arabian Nights, or something like that. It was spectacular. A few years ago I went to the South Street Seaport in New York and realized I was standing on the same dock where we had come into New York in 1964. I bought a model of the boat USS United States across the street in a gift shop. Thank you for your friendship over the years. It has meant a lot to me. I can't tell you what a thrill it was to have you show up in Avignon 21 years ago in your newspaper overalls!

Avignon, July 1999. The 'newspaper overalls' the Doc refers to were part of my final year piece at Dartington College of Arts: *Come Back To Me Then Go Away*. These were white cotton overalls that had diary extracts transfer-printed onto them. The diary entries had been written by a neighbour of mine who had died in a building where I had once rented a bedsit. The landlord had given me permission to video in his flat during 1998 and use anything that had been left as it was all going to be thrown out. I remember in the early 1990s, prior to my cleaning up, being up all night drinking with this neighbour and him saying to me, "Don't waste your life and become an old fart like me". Several years after he died, I was wearing his words as I got into the white Alfa Romero the Doc had hired and we drove through the light Van Gogh had once come here for.

There is a need for the Doc and I to tell each other how much our friendships mean. The clock is on and I wish I'd told Glenn how much his friendship meant to me instead of taking it for granted. I can't recall the last time I'd spoken to Todd. One of the cars we borrowed during the '98 period was a battered blue Honda and we used this to deliver food from a deli over a Jewish holiday in Skokie, the North Shore Chicago suburb. There was a *Back to the Future* quaint Main Street, the flat fronted buildings with little jutting verandas. Some of these householders were real snobs. Of course, it might have been something to do with the car, more New York brusqueness than Chicago approachable. One home we delivered to did invite us in and fed us cinnamon bagels and coffee. They boasted a 60-inch cathode ray tube television that, due to its bulk, had to be housed in its own purpose-built extension. The TV had been won as a prize and the owner had tried to exchange it for a cruise, but it wasn't possible.

Later that evening, Todd gives me a lift to the Uptown Poetry Slam at the Green Mill Lounge where I read as a guest. My pal Glenn had started poetry slams in Bristol in late 1995. The first was at the Arnolfini Gallery on the quayside, opposite where the slave trader Colston's battered bronze statue was unceremoniously dumped in the dock during a Black Lives Matter demonstration. It was through poetry I got to know Glenn as I won the first slam in Bristol. At the Green Mill I met Marc Smith, the construction worker, who started the whole Slam scene and bought two Chicago Poetry Slam T-shirts with a red boxing glove motif from him for $20. I gave one to Glenn when I got back to the UK.

JUST LIKE OLD TIMES

July 1993. Dad drove me from Torquay in a black Ford Sierra with my big canvas hotel laundry bag full of possessions to Barley Wood, a rehab just outside Bristol. This is a journey of nearly 90 miles and it's the last time we'd ever drink alcohol together.

We needed to get comfortable with each other and the legacy of my lifestyle at this time was a default setting of shame and being a fraud. Dad somehow sensed the moment. I always found this conflicting about him, for such a tough guy sometimes he could be quite sensitive. As we drove it got easier, more like old times. "It's about now, son, that's what counts, forget everything else." He lit a Castella Classic cigar and popped in his well-worn tape, *Sinatra at the Sands*.

On my first day at secondary school, I found inside my little zipped blazer pocket a two-shilling piece wrapped in a note that said, 'Good luck, son. Love, Dad xx'. Some mornings after he worked the nightclubs, there would be little square notes and coins for my brother and I on the kitchen table. Little notes with our names on signed, 'Love, Dad'.

I can see his profile now as he pulls the cigar out of his mouth, the broken boxer's nose and sweptback grey Teddy boy hairstyle, wearing his gold ring with the Austrian Ducat. I remember him lifting his fist to a guy one night, "You see this, I'll embed it in your face". None of it matters. The same hand fluttered at the cassette player – "I like that son – turn it up" – as the tempo rises and Frank sings.

I've got you under my skin...

We didn't pass any hitch-hikers on our way towards Bristol but I'm sure if we did he would have given them a lift. Dad was intrinsically a kind man. While we were on the motorway – driving towards, driving away from – it was as if everything was suspended and we were reliving moments from the past without knowing it. Those journeys together during the early 1960s in vans full of fridges smelling of toast and oil; then the cars to the coal yards with the radio on the back-window parcel shelf. I remember the Barnstaple solicitor who phoned my dad for my bail surety way back, telling me he had a Porsche and he'd give me a ride in it. I would have nodded smiling but wouldn't really be interested. It was never about the motors; it was who I shared them with.

The car decelerated as we turned up a slip road and left the motorway, adopting a different rhythm as Dad steered onto country roads, the final part of the journey. It was two-way traffic now and the narrow road focused my apprehension. Dad recognized this and reassured me, "It's going to be alright". We passed long-closed petrol stations and rural scrapyards with the junkers queuing outside, waiting their turn. I gazed at the fields and trees and tried to let go, trying to just accept this was it.

We stopped in a bar in a Somerset village called Churchill, a couple of miles from the rehab. It would have been halves with chasers for me. We drove on mostly in silence to Barley Wood, finally turning off a country lane and up to the premises. We both got out and I heaved the big old laundry bag from the boot. We hugged, Dad kissed my cheek and said, "Just stay here, do what you have to and remember I love you, son". I stood and watched him drive away.

DISTRACTION NUMBER 11

The chrome-collared, bobble-ended curtain pole is at least 12 years old. It has lived with me for over nine of those years, hanging Laura Ashley oatmeal linen curtains lined with blackout material in my 'guest' bedroom. Its rounded finials have borne witness to the vagaries of numerous visitors over the years. The couple of Texan academics of magnificently contrasting stature, who rolled up and hauled their excessive luggage, perceptively reading my face when I met them at Liverpool Street Station. I questioned whether they had their tuxedos with them, which they did, having just finished a world cruise. A spoilt young diplomat's daughter from Switzerland who, when I accompanied her to a gift shop, spoke to the assistant in an abrupt and condescending manner that frankly shocked me. The location of my apartment probably afforded me a little status and my age respect – so she was easy on me. I had looked out for her because she was my daughter's age. The gay Kuwaiti employed by Philip Morris International, who left behind his Armani vest – he told me to give it to charity; I am still wearing it. He texted me late one night during his stay explaining he had sat on the front door key and snapped it. He was at the Notting Hill Carnival and I suspect it had been used to open Red Stripe beer cans. He also had a number of severe nocturnal nosebleeds but did not quibble about buying new

243

pillows. Discussing Middle Eastern politics, he told me Arab states need to be ruled by strong men with a gun.

There was an Israeli couple whose account was registered in Paris. He worked in finance, attending a conference at the Excel Centre. She was charming, but he was a fucking nightmare, his jangling and high-energy vibe pulsed through the walls when he was in the flat. I excelled at non-committal politeness when he denigrated my Muslim Asian neighbours with an arrogant attitude that I'd witnessed in a particular white South African traffic warden in Torquay many years previously. He offered me 'Cognac' emphasizing it was not 'Brandy'. I had experienced both personally and professionally the effects of cocaine and he was displaying all the attributes. I counted the hours until he left. I'd had other guests from this country who were cool; a young film-maker came with me to the opening night of an exhibition by an Iranian/German friend of mine in Dalston. The film-maker and I later took photographs around Spitalfields: a vintage 'Rat' Bentley parked in Elder Street and a plaque on the wall of a house where Mark Gertler, the artist, had once lived. I tried to explain Gertler's Merry Go Round – how things are rarely what they appear to be. Then there was Rosario, an older Italian woman from Monza, who had once lived and worked in London. We stay in touch. Her return will be an indication of pseudo normality.

Things are so fragmented now and I cherish the comfort of friends. In Southwark, I have a particular crew (the contingent) I knock about with, consisting mostly of Italians, Algerian Sid and an extremely hirsute New Zealand photographer. I started to have a tickly cough after a double Macchiato at Capricci. I immediately thought: *Could this be curtains for me?* The niggle might have been exacerbated by the flaky pain au chocolat. I later bought some soothing Ricola (honey herb sweets) and considered the last time I met anyone with a cold.

I notice by Spitalfields Market the traffic still clings to the side of Commercial Street skirting the congestion charge zone and displaying an illusion of one-sided busyness. This too shall pass. The whiff of electro-static ignition and cucumber sanitiser, the fits and starts of a never-quite-achieved new normality. The offices emptying, not just of people, the desks and associated toiling stations ripped out. There is a purpose-built block of 1970s offices next to the Salvation Army headquarters just before the Millennium Bridge. They have a little riverside view, keeping the distractions to a minimum, keeping the workers toiling. Of course, there is the possibility of a residential conversion – but this ain't Croydon, they'll have to do it properly. Back in the loop, knock it down and rebuild. Attract that overseas investment. Silly me, I thought their economies, those overseas investors, were taking a pounding with this Covid malarkey. We're in the loop or is it a bubble?

The comfort of things, especially books. My old friends between the pages, that tell me the old story, *Hard Times* by Studs Terkel always gives me some perspective and helps me realize – relatively – I'm on easy street. The comfort of things in my memory cabinet – tangible objects with associated memories, like the Rose pecan tin retrieved from a Chicago dumpster and presented to me by Darren, an Inuit who lived in a cupboard. The battered back number plate of a 1947 Lincoln Continental registered in Paris and discovered in a field near Grenoble. A lime-green toy Trabant bought in Kreuzberg, Berlin, near an automat photo booth where Louise took a photograph of me wearing my ivory Macintosh – always channelling Michael

245

Caine. Being someone else, somewhere else, but who and where?

I remember the wallpaper mural on Hilda Ogden's wall in the ITV soap serial Coronation Street. In unsubstantial new-build suburban kitchens, colossal wall-mounted flat-screens serve up hyper realistic presenters babbling shite, coming out – no staying in. Babbling through Hollywood teeth while scheming their own exit strategies involving book deals, cake baking, and ballroom dancing. I don't want to get lost in all this. I will come out the other side. Curators and publishers are talking two years while agency staff on zero hours are hoping for May 2021. "You can have £5 today or wait until next week and I'll give you £7."

Unenforceable regulations with exceptions to the rule are the way forward. Everyone has got an excuse, everyone is special. National Service conscription would never work today. There would be objections to selfie sticks on the parade ground and influencers banned from interrogation rooms. I cynically consider the exempt, refracting privilege through the lens of 1980s HIV precautions. I don't remember anyone in the days of HIV grabbing my bloody barrelled syringe and shooting up – trilling: "It's fine, I'm exempt." Not to mention the virus defying bare-back riders.

Stay in – go out. No, it's fine – just put the tip in.

Further – you're either on the bus or off it.

We need a strong man with a gun.

Excuses are truths and you wish they weren't true. People have had enough of this shit but not enough to do anything about it. We're in the loop: Stay in, go out, wear a mask, wash your hands, yeah, wash your hands. Everyone remembers the Pilot.

"Kiss me, pretend I'm someone else – someone good," shrieks the Right Honourable member, caretaking a constituency they couldn't give a flying fuck about while they divvy out the contracts to their chums with names like children's entertainers, who can't be tracked and traced when it comes to accountability. 'Oh, don't be so bitter, strong opinions have no place in here, boy.'

This is the age of the hybrid – half man, half clipboard. Half hope, half App. Soup and a sandwich. Everything to go, click and collect. The sound on the street is Ocado crates stacking on trolleys. The Airbnb wheeled suitcase brigade is just a receding memory. It is so quiet where I live, I'm loath to curtain out the moon. I consider myself a durational performance, occasionally unstable, constantly evolving, morphing lather-lampy like an iTunes visualiser in sensible shoes. How does that work? How does any of this work?

I watch Babylon Berlin online and find myself recalling Cabaret with Liza Minnelli as Sally Bowles. I place Christopher Isherwood swanning through the Duveens Gallery of Tate Britain. A romanticised Weimar Berlin, Mercedes and morphine. A summer scene at the Tiergarten café, fresh-faced Hitler Youth singing 'Tomorrow Belongs to Me' as the potential victims, forking apple strudel, realize the danger of this creeping evil, as the singers get louder and their faces grow harder. All this reminds me of a film I was watching, tripping with the shutters closed in a Victorian villa during the summer of 1974. A black-and-white television with the volume turned down as 'Night Club' by the Scottish band String Driven Thing played on a Garrard SP25 deck. Men were clambering out of shallow water towards a beach and John Wayne was waving from a boat. There were indigenous people on the beach greeting the men and John Wayne was getting angry. I turned the volume up. The clambering men have the plague and Wayne is screaming, "Unclean, unclean!" Things are not what they seem. The churn and the drama

– they don't wrap chips in old newspapers anymore.

Cold War Steve, the British collage artist and satirist with his serial killers, soap stars, and political figures, represents an uncomfortable yet accurate image of dysfunctional and corrupt Britain today. He serves it up as a full English, with the Sleaford Mods providing the soundtrack. No Hilda Ogden panorama – the same scene the serial killers Fred and Rose West posed in front of. These are the days of the democratic visual, like Warhol's *Coca-Cola* and, while you're looking at the colours, the corporations are doing something else – to you. Did you really think it was your decision?

Irene, a diminutive yet efficient security guard, hurriedly entered the gallery in her ankle-high fur-lined boots with her essentials – such as a first aid kit – in small pouches, bouncing off her hips. I always thought she was someone you could rely on in a fix. I had been considering a sneeze as the gallery space was filled with what at first glance were potato sacks, fusty broad-stitched rough-hewn fabrics, shapes that were evocative of cocoon-like forms. The piece was called *Embryology* and was by Magdalena Abakanowicz.

Stern and staring at me, Irene said, "They are drawing penises on the wall!" I couldn't help myself – I pretended not to hear properly to get her to repeat this observation, knowing she is quite pious. 'They are drawing penises on the wall.' I knew the wall she was referring to and the work covering it. *Untitled* by Rudolf Stingel is a wall 5.2 x 9 metres in area, entirely covered with orange Savannah custom colour carpeting. People are invited to draw shapes in the thick pile – a tactile and visual experience. Cocks and the word 'Love' are a regular feature.

I could see Irene in my peripheral vision, awaiting a response. Finally, looking directly at her I said, "With great respect, Irene, if people cannot draw a penis on the wall in Tate Modern – where can they?" With this she nodded in agreement and marched off. My work was done. I'd been thinking about touching and feeling and installations that make you sneeze. My friend Kenneth; an artist and performer, very correctly – he has something of the Derek Jacobi about him – voiced his concern to the health and safety executive (half men, half clipboards) that the orange Savannah custom carpet of roughly drawn cocks was now a possible contagion point. The work is now barriered for our mutual protection.

Back in the late seventies, between The Ramones and – more importantly – Warren Zevon, Brian Eno's *Music for Airports* was the new then. Ambient music is the way forward, exploring a soundtrack for lockdown, for extraordinary times – creating our own atmosphere because there isn't a lot of it outside. I will get the *lumière* right; I want to see everything in the best possible light and finish decorating every room in the flat while exercising and stretching at least five days a week. I detect a fragile yet volatile, simmering violence shimmering like silver static when I walk through Liverpool Street Station. It's not alright and 'Keep Calm and Carry On' posters won't cut it this time. You need to be strong, navigating without charts. Deep waters are better than rocky peninsulas. Your skin gets thinner as you get older. Creating a soundtrack to my life: Noir Ambient, ABBA for exercise, and one hour of melancholic Sovietwave second mix. It's like a railway line running beside the road, racing the train – don't lose your nerve. Trout-pouted, botoxed, drum skin forehead narcissists with their black-blocked eyebrows and lockdown hair, Zooming in tiger onesies while scoffing Uber eats. Under starters orders, home-based hairdressers itch to ask what you're having for tea or where you're going for your holidays – while the static on their visors will collect your split ends. This is all about resources and most definitely mental resources. Remember, hope dies last. Smile with your eyes, do the Duchenne smile. Guillaume-Benjamin-Amand Duchenne, a 19th-century French neurologist, discovered if you electrocute someone's face just right, you can jolt them into smiling. Remember the wind-up electric handshakes?

It is a different world and I ask: Is this the new jazz age? The chaos of inflamed emotions as politicians compete for public attention. I want jazz with my vaccine because this is the time of improvisation, of always staying in the groove, welcoming those contrary collaborations, having faith in the process right through to that resounding applause wafting out the doors of Ronnie Scott's into Frith Street.

Nothing just is. Trapped in a loop of technology and bureaucracy. Incompetent and corrupt governments are the order of the day. No one seems really happy. The passive acceptance of the new normal aiding and abetting constant drifting, dissolving in a Bermudian Triangle of social media. Moving in gangs, when permitted, flexing and whistling in the dark, watching the isolated, distanced aggression of the striding Lone Ranger. Looking back nostalgically, looking forward to nowhere. Everything is so complicated. Putting the mask on, my glasses steaming up, compromising peripheral vision, and missing steps. Everything is so messy and it's easy to drift.

Across the road, Mustafa from Turkey has sold the lease on Jeff's Café where Gilbert and George would frequent some mornings. We would trade stories of Bristol as he'd worked at a café on Stokes Croft near the Banksy *Mild Mild West* Molotov hurling teddy bear – we both knew the area well. Jeff's is now a sushi bar called Honmono. Out of loyalty and frugality, they will never be graced with my presence. Further along on the Tenterground, the now mature YBA Tracey Emin has vacated her studio with its swimming pool in the basement. She's gone up West – more RA than E1 now. She is rich but never bland – no blow-in will top her and long may her initialled rondels stay on her studio – the ones she told me proudly about at a Modigliani exhibition. One morning, standing on the corner of Fournier Street waiting for my friend Andrew the antique dealer to turn up in his white Transit van, I'd got talking to George Parsons, knowing he'd attended Dartington School as a child, when living in Totnes with his mother. I mentioned I had studied at Dartington College of Arts some years previously. As our conversation ended and he walked off toward his house, a woman approached me asking if I'd eaten breakfast that morning. I replied I had but it was very kind of her to ask. I think she was Spanish; I suppose she thought I was tapping George up for a few quid – I was wearing an old leather jacket with a rucksack over my shoulder as we were going to the old Wimbledon dog track car boot sale. This was before a pandemic – this is my London, someone showing such kindness – I have faith it will get better, I believe in people, I will try to be kind. This is peculiar upcycling; I can only hope Gilbert and George go around the corner to the last remaining greasy spoon on Bell Lane; keep a bit of culture handy, if you like.

Gloria, of the Italian contingent, told me it's about stamina – she runs marathons – it's about developing reserves.

Ken Dodd's trademark teeth lost to a mask as he sings 'Tiers for Souvenirs' and I hum 'I'm Still Waiting' by Diana Ross. Big hair and big plans for the future and just maybe we'll learn something, something good. Resilience is the new now. Don't lose the faith and remember: It's a great feeling when you get out.

ACKNOWLEDGEMENTS:

I owe so much to the late Glenn Carmichael, he was not only a dear friend but always supported and inspired me in my writing and performance endeavours.

Louise Burston for her patience, kindness and continual encouragement, Adam Black Stewart for detail, collaboration and friendship, Patrick Wray for becoming an old pal. Harry Harris (the voice of reason) Anthony Turner who planted the seed. My cousins Tina and Lynn for treats and facts.

Richard Jones for being a constant throughout the uncertainty. Sol Wilkinson for seeing the wood for the trees and Jaz Naish for an outstanding cover ("well he would say that").

Especially the Italian contingent (which is really a catch all of a creatively esoteric gang up to and including: Samanta, Max, Federica D & C, Sid, Aaron, Giovanna, Elisa, Agape, Daniel, Gloria, Richard T, Kenneth 'Notes') and all my colleagues at Tate who have enriched my life.

My grateful thanks to all those who have contributed to this story in one way or another.

"When I told Gerry King how much I liked this book he was so pleased he express mailed me his best suit – which he'd grown out of, but it was a perfect fit for me… a very expensive mint condition Christian Dior in a fifties cut. So now I like Gerry just as much as his book!" (*Lubin Tales*)
Stewart Home

"Its writing is as bright, as magical as if Kubrick lit it, its prose warms you with its wit, but the shadow it throws is a truly dark one". (*Smoke and Other Tales*)
**Dr Phil Smith, author of *Mythogeography:*
*A Guide to Walking Sideways***

"I LOVED your book. You have the intensity of Beckett, but totally original work." (*Lubin Tales*)
**Simon Van Booy, author and winner of the
Frank O'Connor International Short Story Award**

"What a life! The painting of a world lived through is vivid, sharp and compelling with some lovely turns of phrase."
**Tim Bouquet, author and feature writer for *The Times
Magazine, Telegraph Magazine* and *Vanity Fair***